Jubilee NOW!
FINAL EDITION

Gidon Ariel and **Bob O'Dell**

Published by
ROOT SOURCE PRESS

ROOT
SOURCE
PRESS

Dedication

To the brave Jewish residents of the Hebron Hills.
— Gidon Ariel

To my wife, Marisa.
— Bob O'Dell

Acknowledgements

We would like to take this opportunity to express our gratitude to the people who supported us, encouraged us, and helped us bring this book to life:

Jebie Piedad, Jayssa Orajay and Arnulfo & Bituin Aquino; Tuly Weisz, Abra Forman, Shlomo Schreibman, Ayal Kellman, and Tsivya Fox of Breaking Israel News; John Bibee and Deborah & Frank Costenbader; and each and every scholar and friend mentioned herein. A special thanks to my wife Devra and **HaKadosh Baruch Hu**.

Endorsements

Gidon Ariel and Bob O'Dell are some of the most interesting thinkers. Their latest quest to discover the "Lost Jubilee" may give us new impetus to pray more for the times in which we live. The valuable points brought out in their new book reminds us that only God can reveal the entire mystery but, through walking together in his pursuit, a way is being paved to grasp new insight we have never had previously presented to us. Their fresh analysis is thought-provoking, as well as, stimulating and intriguing. In a world weighed down with uprisings and unrest, we welcome more understanding of the "mystery" year that may foretell God's intervention to bring freedom and restoration for the planet on which we live. This joint endeavor merits all of us to read the book and decide for ourselves.

SHARON SANDERS
Co-Founder and Director, Christian Friends of Israel, Jerusalem
www.cfijerusalem.org

"Seal the book, even to the time of the end." (Daniel 12:4) Recently during our 19th Passover Conference in Jerusalem, my friends Gidon Ariel and Bob O'Dell spoke, and Bob declared the Jubilee year, calling forth Revival worldwide. Revelations on the Jubilee Year are no doubt part of the unsealing that was prophesied for the End Times in the scroll of Daniel. The research in this book is no doubt part of the End Time unsealing, and I recommend this latest Root Source publication to all, like the children of Issachar, who have understanding of the times!

CHRISTINE DARG
Founder, The Jerusalem Channel
www.jerusalemchannel.tv

This is a very welcomed, scholarly project that will no doubt strengthen Jewish Christian relations in times when both respective groups are being marginalized. It is of significance that a book about Jubilee comes out of Israel from a Jew and Christian partnering together, written to those who love God's Land and His people. I cannot recommend this work highly enough.

FATHER GABRIEL NADDAF
Spiritual leader of the Aramean Christians in Israel
Chairman of the Christian Empowerment Council - the Israeli Christian Recruitment Forum
www.cecisrael.org

God foretold events of the end of the age that were intended to bring hope. That is exactly what Jubilee NOW! offers! Oft-cited gloom and doom topics that fill the pages of Bible prophecy books are given perspective, context, and purpose demonstrating that there is a time of liberation coming, just as God always intended for humanity. Get ready to understand God's purpose of the four blood moons, the Shemitah, and most importantly, the Jubilee – a proclamation of freedom for you, your family, and your nation!

DOUGLAS HAMP
Author, The Millennium Chronicles
www.douglashamp.com

Jewish/Christian relationships were stuck sadly in the deep freeze for 20 centuries. In 2005, when Gidon Ariel began his brave dialogue with the Christian world, he was still a pioneer in this often lonely and neglected field. Thanks to his faithfulness and persistence, Gidon has earned his place at the head of the discussion.

Today, thanks in part to his own efforts, this vital dialogue has become more accepted and much better informed. The partnership between Gidon and Bob has come to personify the true power of Jewish/Christian relations. A heaven-blessed anointing, fresh and sweet, is on all they teach and do together. The exciting revelations they've untapped in this latest book are destined to reverberate throughout the Jewish and Christian worlds.

PASTOR DAVID N. DECKER
President, Acts of Grace
www.actsofgrace.org
Jerusalem, Israel

This latest book by Gidon Ariel and Bob O'Dell on Jubilee is timely and will certainly be thought-provoking to many believers worldwide. The concept of jubilee may be foreign to many Christians but was instituted by G-d Himself. Jubilee is to bring freedom and restoration and is one of the keys to understanding both the Jewish calendar and the Biblical way of living. Again, like their previous one this book too makes the Bible relevant by connecting Jewish and Christian beliefs.

DR. SUSANNA KOKKONEN
Director, Christian Friends of Yad Vashem
www.yadvashem.org

It is incredible what Gidon Ariel and Bob O'Dell have done for Jewish-Christian relations in such a short time. Since launching Root Source just over a year ago, they have already written "Israel FIRST!" and are now publishing their second book, "Jubilee NOW". Their eagerness to move ahead with such energetic passion demonstrates their commitment to pushing forward the important work of strengthening the relationships between Jews and Christians in support of Israel. Some of the ideas in "Jubilee NOW" were developed in articles they published on "Breaking Israel News" and were well received by our readers, so I can be certain that anyone who reads the book will learn many important and fascinating ideas about the Jubilee year.

RABBI TULY WEISZ
Publisher, Breaking Israel News www.breakingisraelnews.com
Director, Israel365 www.Israel365.com
Managing Editor, The Israel Bible www.theisraelbible.com

After more than 26 years of working to bring Jews and Christians together, I am proud to recommend the work of Bob O'Dell and Gidon Ariel and their wonderful organization Root Source. I see them mobilizing an army of wonderful rabbis and teachers who are sharing the values that both Jews and Christians embrace and believe in. Today, Israel, which in my opinion includes Jews and Christians, is being existentially threatened by two primary ideologies: Islam and Atheism, both of which wish to terminate the "Apple of God's Eye," the Jews and Christians together, and as such is a threat to Western Civilization and the human race. Their first book "Israel FIRST!" is just the beginning. This second book, "Jubilee NOW!" is another strong link in a chain, in what I believe will educate, strengthen and protect all those values so dear to all of us.

AVI LIPKIN
Author, Lecturer, Journalist and Founder of the Bible Bloc Party
http://www.vicmord.com/

Jewish history is the story of God's interaction with the Jewish people, working behind the scenes to enable them to accomplish their unique role in history. Within the Torah the concept of the Yovel, or Jubilee, is a powerful symbol of the Jewish people's mission and the ultimate destiny of humanity. Gidon Ariel and Bob O'Dell have researched this concept of the Jubilee thoroughly from many different historical and biblical perspectives. The beauty of the ancient concept of the Jubilee is that it is actively calling for the Messianic age to arrive. With the return of the Jewish people to their homeland and the rebirth of the modern state of Israel, we see the process of redemption — heralding the arrival of the Messianic Age as having already begun, so it is not enough to sit back and wait for The Messiah, we must actively seek ways to improve the world today in order to hasten his coming. I am delighted that Jews and Christians, who share a common belief in this process of the Final Redemption, are coming together to present not only the Jubilee of the past, nor a Jubilee of the future, but a Jubilee for today, the central idea that God is at work in the world to bring us ever closer to His original conception — a Jubilee NOW!

RABBI KEN SPIRO
Author, Senior Lecturer and Researcher
Root Source and Aish HaTorah
www.kenspiro.com

The Jubilee is one example of Israel's being a light unto the nations. Like the Sabbath and the Shemitah Sabbatical Year — the Jubilee reminds us that we are not in charge. God is. We are all His children and more similar than some might think. Just as the concept of a day of rest once a week, which was initiated in the Bible, has been adopted in virtually all societies — we can all benefit by learning about the Jubilee and incorporating its lessons and values in our lives.

I have known Gidon Ariel for many years and am delighted that he has joined up with my new found friend Bob O'Dell to create Root Source, which is truly a blessing for Israel and the world.

RABBI YEHUDAH GLICK, MK
Jerusalem of Peace
http://templemountheritage.com/

בס"ד

Jerusalem, 12 August, 2015
27 Av, 5775

Mr. Gidon Ariel
Founder and CEO of Root Source

Dear friend,

I was glad to hear about the publishing of your new book, "Israel First!" co-written with Bob O'Dell, that offers a thorough examination of the Tanakh and its continued relevance in our time.

Your dedicated efforts throughout the years to deepen the ties with the Christian community around the world through the establishment of an international joint learning site as well as through this book are worthy of the highest esteem. The support that Christian communities lend to the state of Israel is vital to Israel's public diplomacy in particular and to the future of the country in general. An in-depth Tanakh-based study strengthens these relations.

I wish you many more years of fruitful and fulfilling work.

Sincerely,

M.K. Yuli Yoel Edelstein
Speaker of the Knesset

Foreword

It's known as the "Mystery of the Lost Jubilee," and we may now, or very soon, discover the secrets embedded in this prophetic puzzle that began thousands of years ago in the Sinai desert just after the Children of Israel's Exodus from Egypt.

In Leviticus 25:8-10, God announced the Jubilee as a special year, instructing the ancient Israelites to "count off seven Sabbaths of years for yourself, seven times seven years, so that you have the time of the seven Sabbaths of years (49 years)," and to "consecrate the fiftieth year and proclaim a release through the land to all its inhabitants." This, God said, would be the "jubilee for you, and each of you shall return to his own property, and each of you shall return to his family."

For the ancient Israelites, the Jubilee was a year of freedom and restoration — a time that signaled the restoration of their land. Today, for Christians who are grafted into the seed of Abraham and Israel, the Jubilee may signify special blessings — or perhaps something even greater, even world shaking.

If you've read the *The Harbinger* or *The Mystery of the Shemitah* by Rabbi Jonathan Cahn, you'll be familiar with the Year of Jubilee — what Cahn calls the "Super Shemitah" — and the controversy over what exactly it will bring to the world. This 50-year biblical cycle — commonly believed to run from September 2015 to October 2016 — has brought war to the Middle East and the restoration of land to Israel in the past, according to Cahn. In his books, Cahn noted that the two prior seven-year Shemitahs in 2001 and 2008 brought "shaking" to the world's financial markets.

In their first book, *Israel First! Your Key to Understanding the Blood Moons, Shemitah, Promises to Israel, and the Coming Jubilee,* Orthodox

Jew Gidon Ariel and evangelical Christian Bob O'Dell correctly predicted the "lack of a major Shemitah economic collapse" in fall 2015, and argued that whatever land God might "return" to Israel in the following Jubilee year, could be decisive in the relationship between Israel and the world.

Additionally, they found an "80 percent correlation" between prior Shemitahs dating to 1900 and stock market corrections exceeding 20 percent. They believe the appearance of several rare, tetrads of blood moons since 1948 marks the three-phase rebirth of Israel, as well as a three-phase peaking of power in the U.S. and "perhaps western civilization." They proposed that the U.S. is now halfway through a 28-year cycle composed of four seven-year periods that will determine the future of America, arguing Leviticus 26 foretold the "sudden terror" of September 11, 2001 and the decline of power in the U.S. since the global recession of 2008.

Now, in their new book *Jubilee Now!* they delve even deeper into this biblical whodunit and the controversy on whether the Jubilee repeats every 49 years or 50 years — calling into question exactly when the Year of Jubilee actually begins.

If you've been reading all the strange, world-flipping news lately, and asked how it might all fit into biblical end-time predictions, *Jubilee Now!* might blow your mind.

In a series of articles in *Breaking Israel News,* later compiled in *Jubilee Now!,* Ariel and O'Dell invited readers to "become detectives with us — in real life, in a mystery of epic proportions," to solve this unfolding biblical enigma.

On this quest, Ariel and O'Dell promised not to "try to force future events to fit into our preconceived notions."

Without giving away too much, they offered this caveat in the event "nothing happens."

"If we reach December 2017 and nothing substantial has happened, then we may simply have to declare the mystery still unsolved," Ariel and O'Dell wrote.

Given what dozens of prominent prophecy experts we interviewed for *The Babylon Code* view as an unparalleled convergence and acceleration in end-times signs, the "nothing happens" scenario seems rather unlikely.

Of course, only time will tell. Meanwhile, why not embark on the journey to solve "The Mystery of the Lost Jubilee" — a biblical braintwister that could have implications for "the entire world."

As Sherlock Holmes once said, "…when you have eliminated all which is impossible, then whatever remains, however improbable, must be the truth."

~ TROY ANDERSON
Former executive editor of *Charisma* magazine
and co-author of *The Babylon Code*

Table of Contents

Acknowledgements 5

Endorsements 7

Foreword 13

INTRODUCTION 19

PART I

Mystery Defined

  1 An Invitation 27

Case Presented

  2 The Six-Day War 33

  3 Roman Holiday 37

  4 Fifty Is Golden 41

  5 Jewish Jubilee 47

  6 Divine Dilemma 53

Clues Gathered

  7 Judah ben Samuel 59

  8 Prophetic Memories 65

  9 One, Two, Fifty 73

  10 The Back Fifty 79

  11 The Sanhedrin 85

  12 Count Your Blessings 91

History Traced

  13 Blood Moons and Jubilee 97

  14 Jubilee on a Mission 103

  15 Readers Respond 109

  16 Jubilees Across Time 115

Proposition Established

  17 The Eternal Golan 121

  18 Let the Oppressed Go Free 129

  19 Jubilee and Disaster 133

  20 Jubilee and the Return of the Jewish People

       to Their Land 143

PART II

21 Adam's Jubilee 157

22 6,000 Years Old? 165

23 UK's Jubilee and Brexit 171

24 Let's Be Civil 175

25 Why the Tenth Day? 179

26 The Ninth of Av 187

27 The Year of the Lord's Favor 193

28 Finally Found? 199

29 Looking Back—Was 5777 a Jubilee Year? 207

30 A Lady in Waiting 213

31 When Is for You 219

32 Solved 227

Appendix A 237

Appendix B 239

Introduction

"We are living in fascinating times," says pretty much everyone, everywhere, every year in history.

But the argument that people living today are both witness to and players in what just might be the climax and culmination of the world's story seems to be more accepted now than ever before.

As our friends know (and after reading this book, you will be counted among those friends for sure), we, the authors of this book, think that a sign of this is the coming together in friendship of the two faith groups most associated with the God of Abraham, Isaac, and Jacob: Jews and Christians.

Over the past few decades and even more so over the past few years, there has been an explosion of events, articles, symposiums, and simply friendships that are tearing down (if only brick by brick) the walls of separation that have stood between the Jewish People and Christians throughout the centuries. And like a snowball, the more things like this happen, the more there will be others.

As we described in our first book, **Israel FIRST!**, and mention in the current volume, this phenomenon has detractors on both sides of the aisle, but we, the co-authors of both of these books, feel very strongly that there is no turning back: God's will is that all of His children come together to give Him glory, and that realization is now more clear than ever and growing clearer constantly.

Why *Jubilee NOW!*

In our last book, *Israel FIRST! The Key to Understanding the Blood Moons, Shemitah, Promises to Israel, and the Coming Jubilee,* we laid out our theory about how all of these components come together to shed light on what God is doing in Israel and in the whole world, and how in fact Israel is a light tower for God's plans. These plans call for Christians and all God-fearers to turn to Him and especially to focus on their relationship with His people, Israel, the Jewish people.

Today, the year after the Shemitah is upon us, it is our responsibility to explore and delve deeply into the concept of the Jubilee, the Yovel, and try to understand what God means for us to know and do.

This is especially important as, in contrast to Shemitah and Blood Moons, there are barely any books written for Christians about the Jubilee. We are humbled that God has left this field wide open for us so to speak, and accept this mission to seriously introduce this critical topic to the world.

What to Expect

As we explain in Chapter 1, the Jubilee is truly a mystery. In this book, we do our best to approach this mystery from all sides, and we invite you to join us for the ride, taking as active a part as you feel comfortable doing.

The name we gave this book, **_Jubilee NOW!_**, rings back to its predecessor, _Israel FIRST!_ While the book begins somewhat tentatively, your confidence will begin to build as Jubilee-like events begin happening, your questions increase through many twists and turns, and your awe will rise to a marvelous crescendo when the mystery is finally declared solved, but in surprising and unexpected ways! Our title **_Jubilee NOW!_** became a prayer that was ultimately answered.

Furthermore, this book is addressed to you, our reader, and all people of the world, encouraging you to focus on the Jubilee and its lessons now. While some of this book's chapters are based on chapters in our first book, the lion's share were published originally as op-ed pieces on the popular website, www.BreakingIsraelNews.com. We take this opportunity to thank its publisher Rabbi Tuly Weisz and his great team for hosting us there.

INTERACTIVE

As we emphasize over and over, the most important value we at Root Source have is relationship. That is why in every article we publish, we invite our readers to comment and enter into a discussion with us. To bring this point home, we have included some of those comments here in this book! While commenting on Internet articles is a well-known characteristic of Web 2.0, the Social Web, we go one step further and incorporate comments in our printed book! If you commented on any of the first 18 articles we published on Breaking Israel News, look for your comment here. And if you would like to comment further, just go to the dedicated page on our website, http://www.root-source.com/blog/jubilee-book-discussion/. Disclaimer: Just like the Internet, each comment reflects the opinion of its author and not necessarily the authors of Jubilee NOW! In fact, if a comment sounds a little crazy to you, we probably agree:-) But our policy on relationships calls for open doors, and if any comments are offensive to you, we encourage you to just skip to the next one.

Another innovation that this book embraces is "POD," which stands for Print On Demand. This means that instead of printing a thousand or more books upfront, each copy is created especially for you, and any errors found can be corrected in subsequent books in the same edition! This means that if you find any typos, please notify us and thanks to you we will make a better reading experience for those who come after you.

WHO ARE THE AUTHORS?

This book is quite unusual in that it is a cooperative effort of Gidon Ariel — an Orthodox Jew — and Bob O'Dell, an evangelical Christian. In the process of developing and revealing their perspective on Jubilee to tens of thousands of Christians worldwide, what fascinated them was the striking alignment of the Jewish and Christian conclusions reached in this book concerning Israel and the rest of the world. Regarding the future, the concept of Messiah is central to Jewish belief. While Jews and Christians may not agree on the Messiah's identity, they are in full agreement that the Messiah is coming and worthy of eager anticipation.

Because this book is written primarily for Christians, Gidon has given Bob complete freedom to write his chapters about Christian concepts in a way that fully proclaims Christian faith, so no Christian teaching is watered down. Naturally, such passages are Bob's work and not Gidon's. Similarly, passages that describe the traditional Jewish perspective which are not in line with Christian theology are Gidon's

Bob and Gidon by Jaffa Gate in Jerusalem

alone. So, while this book might ruffle a few feathers on both sides of the religious aisle, it advances the building of bridges between these two related faiths.

Gidon Ariel

Gidon Ariel is the co-founder and CEO of Root Source. Gidon made *Aliyah* (return to the Holy Land) in 1978 at age 14, and spent close to a decade in advanced Jewish studies institutes (*Yeshivas*) and the Israel Defense Forces (IDF). Raised as an Orthodox Jew and still an observant Jew, Gidon has kept Jewish traditions his entire life. Quite unexpectedly, in 2005 he felt a personal call from *Hashem* (God) to begin to reach out to Christians in friendship and to bless and educate them about Jewish life, thought, and insights about Hebrew Scriptures. After spending much time working with Christian individuals and organizations in Israel and around the world, Gidon came to see that Jewish concern about getting "too friendly with Christians" is largely unfounded. He sees God calling upon Jews and Christians to come together in relationships and to find ways to work together based on the truth of the Bible. Gidon still serves in the IDF reserves as a captain in the Military Spokesperson's Office after spending over 20 years in the Armored Tank Corps. Besides being CEO of Root Source, Gidon teaches Jewish Prayer and the Leadership of Moses on Root Source. He can be reached at gidon@root-source.com.

Bob O'Dell

Bob O'Dell is a non-Jewish Christian and a former high-tech executive with Motorola and Wintegra. He has worked with Israeli Jews for over 25 years, visiting Israel over 40 times since 1990. Bob founded Root Source with Gidon Ariel to promote Gidon's vision of Israeli Jews teaching Christians worldwide. Bob's perspective of his Jewish roots has changed through direct contact with Israeli Jews like Gidon and through other Root Source teachers and their study of the Hebrew Scriptures. An astronomy enthusiast for more than 35 years, Bob was the first to reveal that the March 20, 2015, Total Solar Eclipse's shadow would cross the North Pole for two minutes at sunrise on the first day of spring for the first time in 100,000 years. Gidon and Bob jointly called for two minutes of prayer worldwide that "the earth would be full of the knowledge of the Lord as the waters cover the sea" (Isa.11:9). Bob attends an evangelical church in Austin, Texas. He can be reached at bob@root-source.com.

WHAT IS ROOT SOURCE?

Today, more and more Christians and Jews are hearing a divine wake-up call to engage with each other.

Root Source is answering that call. In an informal and loving manner, scholarly Orthodox Israeli Jews teach Christians around the world online about Jewish concepts, ideas, and thoughts to help Christians understand the roots of their faith.

Root Source enables and encourages dialogue and relationships between Christians and Jews, and empowers Christians to learn as Jews have been learning for centuries. Our Israeli Jewish teachers respect the identity and faith of their Christian students.

Root Source gives Christians access to world-class Jewish biblical teaching online, helping them learn deeper truths and reach higher in their Christian faith, with the opportunity to ask questions openly.

Our members are often surprised at how quickly they can learn deeper biblical truths from Orthodox Jewish teachings and practically apply those teachings to their own Christian faith.

Current courses cover topics such as:

- Jewish Prayer
- Jewish History and Future
- Biblical Hebrew
- Women of the Bible
- Leadership of Moses
- Solomon's Proverbs
- Chapters of the Fathers
- Land of Israel
- Understanding Islam
- The Holy Temple
- Names and Images of God
- Blood Moons and More
- Jubilee

Learn more at www.root-source.com.

CHAPTER 1

An Invitation

What if we told you that there was a mystery right in front of us? A mystery that is not just imaginary but real, a mystery that when solved could have implications to the entire world. Would you be interested to read such a story? More than that, would you be interested to join in with such a story?

What we are about to embark upon could be every bit as exciting as a Sherlock Holmes mystery novel. Everyone loves a good mystery novel! We get caught up in the writer's story, identifying with the characters as they seek to solve the mystery in front of them. But when the book ends, the adventure also ends. A book can be a needed escape, perhaps, but then we must go back to real life.

But we would like to offer you something different. To become detectives with us, in real life, in a mystery of epic proportions.

Which mystery? Not the mystery of when the Messiah will appear! Yes, that is the most important mystery of all, but let us agree that such a mystery can be left to many others, and has defeated many a detective over the years.

No, the mystery we propose to work on together is the Mystery of the Lost Jubilee. We propose that we work together in the coming chapters and to communicate with each other through modern social media in order to try to solve it.

This mystery novel, we would suggest, is a novel being written by God and all Bible-believing people are characters in the novel, and all are invited to be detectives if they choose to be. We — Bob, an evangelical Christian from America and Gidon, an Orthodox Jew from Israel — are co-authoring this book together. This mystery is most certainly a shared mystery, of great interest to Jews and Christians alike.

To "find the lost Jubilee" is to definitively find any Jubilee, and then to definitively find a second Jubilee, and then with that pattern established, solving the mystery means finding all Jubilees to come. If we are in a Jubilee year right now, **and we were all to agree upon it**, then we may have just solved the mystery. But, we are a long way from understanding the possibilities, or agreeing with the evidence, evidence which we have not even begun to present just yet, but which we will present bit by bit in the book you are holding — physical, historical and biblical evidence.

If things go well, we might be able to solve the Mystery of the Lost Jubilee as early as Spring 2016, and if not perhaps by Summer or Fall of 2016, but — and here is the best part — we have a lot of confidence that, with God's help, together we should all be able to propose a definitive solution to the Mystery of the Lost Jubilee no later than by the end of 2017.

Suppose we find it. So what? What does finding the Lost Jubilee imply for our world? We begin by establishing a few simple facts that those who have studied the Jubilee will already know.

What is the Jubilee?

The Jubilee is a special year that was instituted by God thousands of years ago when it was announced to the children of Israel in the Sinai desert just after their Exodus from Egypt. It is instituted in scripture in Leviticus 25:8-10:

> *You are also to count off seven sabbaths of years for yourself, seven times seven years, so that you have the time of the seven sabbaths of years, namely, forty-nine years. You shall then sound a **ram's horn***

*abroad on the tenth day of the seventh month; on the day of atonement you shall sound a **horn** all through you land. You shall thus consecrate the fiftieth year and proclaim a release through the land to all its inhabitants. It shall be a **jubilee** for you, and each of you shall return to his own property, and each of you shall return to his family.* (emphasis added)

A Jew blowing a shofar (Photo: Wikimedia Commons)

The English word "jubilee" in verse 10 in Hebrew is pronounced "yovel" and literally means "a ram's horn." The ram's horn and horn mentioned in verse 8 is pronounced "shofar," which is itself ram's horn.

Why is the Jubilee important?

The Jubilee is a year of freedom and restoration. But beyond that, since it is a year that is consecrated to the Lord, the time of Jubilee hints at heavenly participation in earthly freedom and restoration.

Why should Jews and Christians care?

Jews in Israel may have restored during a Jubilee something critically important to their national identity, namely *physical land*. Christians are grafted into the seed of Abraham and Israel, so the Jubilee can bring, at the very least, spiritual blessings to Christians even as it brings, at the very least, physical blessings to the Jews.

When does Jubilee occur?

God explains that it is to be the 50th year, occurring after seven 7-year long cycles. There is great controversy about whether this fiftieth Jubilee repeats every 49 years or 50 years. We will study this later, but if our overall objective of together finding the Lost Jubilee is met, we should be able to answer this question once-and-for-all.

Is any specific year designated as the Jubilee Year by the Jews?

No, not officially, although interest to identify this year has been growing among Jews recently. There are many obstacles to an official recognition of the Jubilee in Israel today, the first of which is that lack of recognized boundaries for what land belonged to which of the twelve tribes. We will cover this more detail in this book.

Was Jubilee observed in ancient Israel?

Not that we know of. We do not possess any definitive evidence of such observance.

Is Jubilee recognized by Christians?

Not in general, except by the Catholic Church, which is coincidentally declaring a Jubilee year to begin on December 8th, 2015! We will discuss this in Chapter 3.

How will we solve this mystery?

By praying, watching, and sharing our insights together. We will pray for God's will to be done regarding the Jubilee; we will watch to see what happens on the earth; and we will share with each other our thoughts in the comments section following each article in this series. If God decides, he can make it very obvious to all of us that a Jubilee year has occurred. We will see it with our own eyes, and hear it with our own ears. It should be that obvious.

And what if nothing happens?

If we reach December 2017 and nothing substantial has happened, then we may simply have to declare the mystery still unsolved. Our promise to you is that we won't try to force future events to fit into our preconceived notions. Detectives follow the evidence wherever it leads, even if it means they have to go back to the beginning and start over.

This is where real life differs from a novel. If we read a good mystery novel, we are guaranteed to reach a meaningful conclusion by the end of the book. In our case, God has no obligation to grant us the right to solve a mystery in any certain time period.

We have no guarantees! But the rewards are real, not imaginary. And the Bible says in Proverbs 25:2 that it is the glory of God to conceal a matter, but the glory of kings to search it out.

We therefore to humbly invite you to join us in treasure hunt! **Would you like to put your detective skills at work, and jump into this story with us?** Shall we try to search it out together, as Jews and Christians who share a common interest in the outcome?

As the authors, we will gather together for you, in this book, all the main facts and clues that have been written about the Jubilee, especially those hints that appear in the Bible. We will also review the facts and clues you provide as well! Together we will attempt to solve this mystery, by finding a treasure not hidden in the ground, but hidden in *time*, the Mystery of the Lost Jubilee.

Timothy Tyler Herschell

Not sure what good I could contribute but... Count me in!

Sheila Demetrus

I am so ready for this! Count me in!

Kevin Dillon

Christian Steep might be able to help you solve this mystery at Facebook "seventy x seven"

Matt Wilson

Count me in.

All nations should observe the Shemitah and Jubilee years. Why?

Mathematically, nations work like snow falling on a mountain. Stability is an illusion. Crashes will always come. The only way to eliminate big crashes is by having lots of little ones - the Shemitah and Jubilee years.

CHAPTER 2

The Six-Day War

In the last chapter, we invited you to join us as we work together like detectives to solve the Mystery of the Lost Jubilee. Solving the mystery means finding a treasure, not hidden in the earth, but hidden in *time*, discovering when this mysterious year may have occurred in the past, the present and when it will occur in the future.

We said we hoped that we might be able to solve this mystery together sometime in 2016 or at least by the end of 2017, and we asked you to write the comment "Count me in" if you wanted to jump into the detective story with us, no prior Jubilee experience required! More than one hundred followers joined us then.

Why are people getting excited about the years 2016 and 2017 in connection with the Jubilee?

The answer has to do with certain events of the past.

Let us go back to spring of 1967 in Israel. Fear was mounting within the nation as enemy forces gathered against the tiny country. Jordan, Egypt and Syria were preparing to attack. Jordan controlled the West Bank, the Old City of Jerusalem and everything up to the line drawn in thick green magic marker in the armistice agreements of 1949; Egypt controlled the Sinai Peninsula; and Syria held the Golan Heights. Then, between June 5 and June 10, Israel waged the famous and miraculous Six-Day War, taking these territories from the belligerent Arab states.

The victory was unexpected by everyone, not only in the territory gained but by the speed in which the war was decided and the relatively light casualties incurred by Israel compared to the Arabs they fought.

Twenty Arab soldiers died for every Israeli, uncommon especially because the Israeli Defense Forces (IDF) was the army gaining territory, not the other way around.

Besides the massive land gains in the Golan Heights, Judea and Samaria, and Sinai, the most important result was the reunification of the entire city of Jerusalem into Israel's hands, which soon would be declared its "Eternal Capital." This war changed so many things, and set so many wheels in motion which still spin today — the rise of a more stable and defendable Israel with the reclamation of critically important lands for its own defense, and the restoration of the Western Wall as a place of prayer. Along with this came the rise of opposition to Israel and the seed of the narrative of Israeli occupation of the West Bank, the popularization of the term "Palestinian" to replace "Arab," the birth of opposition to international recognition of Jerusalem as Israel's capital, the beginning of the withdrawal of each and every national embassy previously present in Jerusalem, and much more.

Jerusalem: The Eternal Capital of Israel (Photo: Bob O'Dell)

Of course we, Gidon and Bob, see all this as the having the fingerprints of God/Hashem. God sought to make good on His covenant to bring the Jews back into the Land of Israel. And this leads us to make an extremely important assumption: *this detective story assumes that God is in control and is an active participant in world affairs*, and that together, we are trying to search out and discover God's intentions, to understand His future actions. While we will try to keep an open mind about many things, this is one major assumption that must we state right away!

The establishment of the Jewish State of Israel occurred on May 14, 1948, and the world witnessed a "nation born in a day" literally fulfilling Isaiah 66:8. The Six-Day War in 1967 marked the beginning of a new era for the nation of Israel. Those events in 1967 were and still are so significant, that it marks the first historical clue of our detective work. Even without any additional supporting facts (of which there are many), it is enough to compel us all to watch carefully the events that might happen 49 or 50 years later to see if God will "do it again!"

Without explaining the significance of the Hebrew Calendar and the Shemitah cycles (which we will examine in future chapters), a simple calculation follows. Given that there is a debate regarding whether Jubilee years occur every 49 years or every 50 years, and considering the importance of the events of the Six-Day War (when the nation of Israel doubled in size in a week), it behooves us to add 49 and 50 to 1967.

And the answers are: 1967 + 49 = 2016 and 1967 + 50 = 2017.

So there you have it! This simple observation of the monumental importance of the Six-Day War in Israel's history, together with the addition of 49 and 50 gives us two very important years to watch! So we need to start our detective work right now!

Questions for discussion and thought

Now does it make sense to you now, why so many people are watching 2016 and 2017?

If God were to do something amazing for the nation of Israel in 2016 or 2017, what might **you** want it to be?

And conversely, if you do **not** think that God is actively involved in the affairs of modern Israel, why not?

Steven P Manos

If God were to do something amazing for the nation of Israel in 2016 or 2017, what might YOU want it to be? I would most like to see them recognize Jesus their Messiah. Next I would like to live to see God restore to them the promised land from the Brook of Egypt to the River Euphrates.

Dianne Witzell

When Israel recognizes Jesus as their Messiah, they will be calling Him Yeshua -- His Hebrew name.

Dixie Vangelisti

Steven Manos, I to have that same desire for GOD'S people. The ROSE of SHARON by any other NAME is still THE ROSE. JESUS was also called

THE NAZARENE. I love that NAME. Spoken in any language "JESUS" was and is

and always will be THE NAME ABOVE ALL NAMES. HalleluJAH!!!!

Dianne Witzell I know many Jews who call the SON of GOD JESUS because they speak english. Hope that's okay.

Charles Foster

Dianne Witzell ...or Yahoshua...or Mashiach...or Isa al Mesih if they are Arab speaking Jews...but trust me Dianne, The Son of the living God of Abraham, Isaac, Jacob will answer when you call ANY of His beautiful Names. None of them are offensive to Him, so let's not introduce offense when none need exist.

LeAnn Giberson

Stephen P Manos has expressed my hopes for Israel...that all of Israel will recognize Jesus as their Messiah and be saved. That was the apostle Paul's prayer as well. I look forward to the day when the Jewish people and gentile Christians will join hands and worship God in spirit and in truth through His Son Jesus Christ. Even so, Father for so it seems good in your sight. Amen.

Quick question: Why is the Gregorian calendar being followed for the Jubilee year? My understanding is that Jubilee should follow soon after the Jewish New year, which would make it late 2015 or late 2016. Please address this. Thanks.

CHAPTER 3

Roman Holiday

In the previous chapter, we discussed the significance of the year 1967 to the Jewish people and Israel; that being the reunification of Jerusalem and its establishment as the eternal capital of Israel. We then added 49 and 50 years to that date, suggesting that 2016 and 2017 are critical years to watch closely.

But what about non-Jews?

Among all of Christianity, the Catholic Church has invested more energy and focus into the concept of Jubilee than anyone else. And the *Catholic Jubilee* year began on December 8th 2015! How did that decision come about?

The first Jubilee year in Christianity has been generally regarded to be the year 1300, when Pope Boniface VIII declared that year to be the one when the church would be offering full pardon and forgiveness of sins to those who travel to Rome and confess their sins. While the word *jubilee* never appeared in the papal declaration (it used the term *celebration*), before long this year began to be referred to in writings of that era as the Jubilee Year.

While the pope's intention was that the next such year be a full one hundred years later, Pope Clement VI declared that the next Jubilee would occur in 1350. That celebration was so popular that new Jubilee dates began to be declared by the church in various years as follows.

- 1390 (40 years after 1350)

- 1400 (50 years after 1350)

- 1423 (33 years after 1390 in commemoration of the life of Christ)

– 1450 (because that was 50 years after 1400)

– 1475 (Jubilees now began to be declared every 25 years!)

The 25 year pattern continued until 1900, when things began to get complicated again.

– 1900

– 1933 (33 years after 1900)

– 1950 (50 years after 1900)

– 1966 (33 years after 1933)

– 1983 (Extraordinary)

However, in 1983, Pope John Paul II declared a Jubilee outside of the normal pattern, an extraordinary Jubilee called the Holy Year of Redemption. Since then, Jubilee years can be declared by the pope in addition to any regular interval, such as the regular Jubilee that occurred on the year 2000.

In April 2015, Pope Francis declared that an extraordinary Jubilee would begin on December 8, 2015, which marks the start of the Catholic Church's yearly calendar. This year would be celebrated as the Year of Mercy. The most talked about provision of this Year of Mercy within Catholic circles is the ability for Catholic priests to directly forgive the sin of abortion, without having to refer the matter to a church bishop.

Pope Francis said it was no accident that he decided that this Jubilee Year was to begin exactly 50 years from the closing of the Second Vatican council. Vatican II addressed the relationship between the Catholic Church and the modern world, including a brief statement rejecting anti-semitism. "Mercy," said the pope, "relates us to Judaism and Islam, both of which consider mercy to be one of God's most important attributes." However, after the Paris attacks of November 13, additional work was underway to secure the large throngs of pilgrims in Rome from being attacked by radical Islamists.

St. Peter's Basilica (Photo: Emilio Garcia, Wikicommons)

There is certainly no conscious connection between the Pope's declaration of the Catholic Year of Mercy, December 8, 2015 through November 20, 2016, and our search for a Jubilee year that might be silently repeating throughout history. The Pope can call a Jubilee whenever he wishes.

But what about the opposite argument? Might the selection of this year by the pope be evidence *against* its selection by God? We raise this question because Christians have such widely differing views of the papacy.

We feel no need to weigh in on that matter here, because the answer doesn't affect the outcome. Proverbs 21:1 gives us a clue:

The king's heart is in the hand of the Lord, as the rivers of water: he turneth it whithersoever he will. (KJV)

So the question is not "what is the Pope doing?" It is "what is *God* doing?"

Questions for discussion and thought

Is God sovereignly directing the events of the Catholic Church, such that Pope Francis declares a Jubilee year exactly 49 years from the Six-Day War in 1967 when Jerusalem was reunited to Israel?

Is God more likely to restore something important to Israel during a year that Catholics also are looking for mercy from God and declaring a Jubilee?

Hudson Steele

The leadership of all nations is instilled by G-d. He will use all, evil or righteous, to further His own plans and outcomes. G-d allows satan to control those who do evil, so that His plans for the world come to fruit Perhaps you should read Job 1:6 Now the day came about, and the angels of God came to stand beside the Lord, and the Adversary, too, came among them. 7 The Lord said to the Adversary, "Where are you coming from?" And the Adversary answered the Lord and said, "From going to and fro on the earth and from walking in it." Now I went to and fro throughout the entire earth and I did not find anyone like Abraham, about whom it is said (Gen. 13:17): "Rise, go to and fro in the land." The Sages of blessed memory (Baba Bathra 16a) said that the Adversary meant this for the sake of Heaven, in order that Abraham's merit not be forgotten by our God.

Hudson Steele

Job is one of my favorites.

Greg Spears

A catholic jubilee means nothing. It will amount to nothing, The 10th Jubilee for the Jews is the one to watch and watch closely.

Sheila Dale

I'm not familiar with the concept of 'the 10th jubilee'. Can you point me to a website for additional information? Thanks

Jeri Carter

Greg Spears;you might look at 120 jubilees; MULTIPLE 50 YEARS WITH 120 JUBILEE'S AND YOU GET 6,000 YEARS. Something to think about

CHAPTER 4

Fifty Is Golden

In the last chapter, we discussed the decision by Pope Francis to call an extraordinary Jubilee for the Catholic Church's yearly calendar beginning December 8, 2015.

Let us now add to the Catholic perspective on Jubilee, a secular perspective and a Protestant one.

The term Jubilee has long been associated with 50-year celebrations. Nation states are said to reach their Golden Jubilee in their fiftieth year of existence. The Republic of Singapore, the island nation that won its independence from Malaysia in 1965, just finished theirs. They began to celebrate as soon as their fiftieth year began, ending with a grand Golden Jubilee celebration on the fiftieth anniversary of independence, August 9, 2015. Israel celebrated its fiftieth year of independence in 1998, but did not formally call it a Jubilee celebration.

Kings and queens are said to reach their Golden Jubilee in their fiftieth year of reign. In recent years these have included Queen Elizabeth II of the United Kingdom in 2002, King Rama IX of Thailand in 1996, and Emperor Hirohito of Japan in 1976. Queen Victoria of the United Kingdom, for whom the Victorian era is named, celebrated her Golden Jubilee in 1887 with the invitation of 50 European kings and princes to a grand banquet.

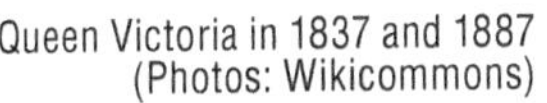

Queen Victoria in 1837 and 1887
(Photos: Wikicommons)

The term *jubilee* is not only used in connection with fifty year celebrations. Common anniversaries that have borrowed the term jubilee are:

- Silver Jubilee: 25 years
- Ruby Jubilee: 40 years
- Golden Jubilee: 50 years
- Diamond Jubilee: 60 or 75 years
- Platinum Jubilee: 70 or 75 years

For the most part Protestant Christianity has adopted the same usage of the word jubilee as the secular world: it is simply a 50-year celebration. A married couple celebrates their fiftieth year of marriage as their Jubilee year. A church or ministry celebrates its Jubilee year. We celebrate the accomplishments of the past, and try to envision what the next 50 years might bring.

But, while all Jubilee celebrations embody the elements of both the *closing* out of a period of years and the *opening* of a new span of years, the foundational Jubilee verse in Leviticus 25:10 calls for more than just *celebration*. It calls for *return*.

*Consecrate the fiftieth year and proclaim liberty throughout the land to all its inhabitants. It shall be a jubilee for you; each of you is to **return** to your family property and to your own clan.* (NIV, emphasis added.)

The Hebrew word for "return" here is *shuv* meaning to turn, turn back, repent, or return. This word is used hundreds of times in the Bible and is the same word used famously as "turn" in 2 Chronicles 7:14:

*If my people, who are called by my name, will humble themselves and pray and seek my face and **turn** from their wicked ways, then I will* *hear from heaven, and I will forgive their sin and will heal their land.* (NIV, emphasis added.)

I propose that if there is a connection between Protestant Christianity and the Jubilee, it will be found in the spiritual activities that underlie the Jubilee. In other words we must look for activities involving "turning," "repentance," or "return." Where might we look?

Why don't we start by looking to the world's most famous non-Catholic Christian. Who is he?

He appeared on Gallup's list of the world's most admired men over 50 times, and for a stretch of 49 consecutive years! He has preached to over 2 billion people in his career. This person is Billy Graham of course, who turned 97 on November 7, 2015.

Billy Graham's organization continues today under the leadership of his son Franklin Graham, who also runs Samaritan's Purse. Franklin Graham took what I consider to be his boldest step yet in his leadership of the Billy Graham Evangelical Association, announce a special year-long series of gatherings in all 50 states in the U.S. in 2016, called the Decision America Tour, www.decisionamericatour.com.

While this event has not been connected to the term *jubilee* by Franklin Graham himself, the substance of this large effort ties directly to the "return" principle of the Jubilee. The first goal and action of the Decision America Tour is to call Christians in the United States to pray and repent – to turn back to "the Almighty God and His Son Jesus Christ" which Graham strongly states is the "the only hope for this country." Note the unspoken reference to Jubilee:

- The repentance focus in 2 Chronicles 7:14 and the word "turn" (*shuv*)
- That 50 States will be visited

- That all gatherings will conclude in 2016, presumably before the American elections in November

The pope has called for a Jubilee year in 2016, including a special emphasis on forgiveness of sin. Now the Billy Graham organization initiates a year-long focus on repentance before the election of the leader of the free world, the president of the United States of America. Are these two major announcements for yearlong activities in 2016 a coincidence?

When were these initiatives decided? That we do not know, but we know when they were announced. Pope Francis made his declaration on April 11, 2015. Graham's announcement followed just four days later. On the Jewish calendar, the pope's announcement was one week after Passover, the last day of the Feast of Unleavened Bread, also known within Jewish circles as the "Festival of Freedom."

It begs the question, is all this coincidence, or is God trying to get our attention?

One thing is for sure: millions of Christians are being primed to consider the coming year as important, whether Catholic or not. Should major changes happen in 2016 or 2017, it is conceivable, depending on what happens, and how it happens, that millions of people might connect the Jubilee, or at least the principles behind it, to those changes.

Why does it matter if millions of people notice something important? Because when God does a significant work on the earth, it is not intended for just a few, but for all. Isaiah 11:9 says:

...for the earth shall be full of the knowledge of the Lord, as the waters cover the sea. (KJV)

God gives many hints of His work, so that many people in different locations, with diverse nationalities and backgrounds may have the opportunity to witness it. Even though no one can see all of His workings, each will see it from a slightly different perspective.

Regarding the Decision America Tour, is this the first 50-state prayer tour ever held in the United States? Certainly not. Is the United States the only focal point for God's work? Absolutely not, and neither is Rome. Is 2016 the first year God has called us to repent and turn to Him? Certainly not. Even if 2016 turns out to be a special and pivotal year, it will only be so because of all the prayer work that has preceded it. The question is rather:

Will 2016 or 2017 mark a *return (or turning point, repentance)* of epic proportions in the Christian world?

Questions for discussion and thought

If God were to appoint 2016 or 2017 to be years of *return* in the Christian world, what might that look like?

Do you have an interesting 50-year Jubilee story to tell? What special thing has God done as it relates to a fiftieth year of marriage, 50 years for your community, your life, your church, your synagogue, etc?

LeAnn Giberson

I love the emphasis on a spiritual jubilee...indeed 'to return' is what it's all about. Come, let us return to the Lord (Hosea 6:1).

Ralf Meister

Repentance and return would most certainly be nice. I would say the surest sign of this actually happening would be if the Ten Commandments would be obeyed and carried out again within the church.

CHAPTER 5

Jewish Jubilee

In the last chapter, Bob discussed the secular and Protestant Christian perception of the Jubilee. In this article, we return to Israel, and I, Gidon, will briefly explain the Orthodox Jewish perception.

Since the re-establishment of the state of Israel 67 years ago, not much attention within the religious Jewish community in Israel has been paid to re-establishing the Jubilee. I believe this may be changing, but first, let me explain how the Jubilee is generally understood by Orthodox Jews.

What is the Jubilee?

The word itself has very clear origins in biblical Hebrew. It is the Greek/Latin transliteration of the Hebrew word *yovel*. The "y" became a "j", the "o" became a "u", the "v" became a "b", and a double-e was tacked on at the end. Yovel seems to be an alternate word for shofar.

The word *yovel* appears several times in the Torah, but by far the most frequent use is in these verses of Leviticus 25:8-13:

You shall count seven Sabbatical years — seven years seven times — until the seven Sabbatical years come to 49 years. And you shall pass [likely meaning blow] the sound of a shofar on the tenth day of the seventh month, on Yom Kippur you shall blow the shofar in all your land. And you shall sanctify the fiftieth year and proclaim freedom in the land for all its residents — it shall be a Jubilee (yovel) for you, each man will return to his ancestral property, and each man will return to his family. This fiftieth year will be a Jubilee year for you — you shall not plant and you shall not harvest what grows, and you shall not harvest the vines. For it is a Jubilee, it will be holy to you — from the field you shall eat the produce. During the Jubilee each man will return to his ancestral property. (English translation by Gidon Ariel)

The Jubilee is the fiftieth year of the Shemitah cycle. In fact, it isn't really correct to call it the Shemitah cycle to begin with. It is really the Jubilee cycle, which is made of seven Shemitah cycles.

The Jubilee year is culmination of this 49-year cycle. It is a year-long commemoration of the completion of the old and the beginning of the new. The event that sets off the Jubilee is the blowing of the shofar on Yom Kippur. This, more than anything else, distinguishes the Jubilee from the rest of the years of the cycle. It is a very public and very national proclamation of a restart of society: slaves are freed, property is restored to its original owners, and the calendar is set back to zero.

How should the Jubilee be observed?

The answer is in the details of the four activities associated with the Jubilee, mentioned in the Torah. These are:

1. **Blowing the shofar on Yom Kippur.** This likely resembled the ceremony that is still observed today on Rosh Hashanah. The Mishnah, the oldest recorded document of the Jewish oral tradition concerning Jewish law, states explicitly that the two are the same.

2. **Freeing slaves.** This is exactly what is says. Thankfully, slavery is an aspect of biblical Judaism that was not continued beyond the biblical period, as far as we know. Consequently, this aspect of the Jubilee would probably be irrelevant, even if the commemoration of the year would somehow be reinstituted in modern times.

3. **Restoring property to its original owner.** The land of Canaan

was divided up between families according to the twelve tribes of Israel. Each family owned a specific plot, granted to be their ancestral land forever. Even if some or all of that land was sold or ownership transferred in some other way (for instance, as a donation to the Temple), the land would be restored to the descendants of the original owner when the Jubilee year came around. Most of the details in both the Torah and the Mishnah concerning the Jubilee concern this particular aspect.

4. **Observing the agricultural restrictions as in a Shemitah year.** Based on a simple reading of the Torah, this implies that there are two years in a row of restricted agricultural activity — the seventh Shemitah year and the Jubilee year which follows it. Presumably, the promise of a bountiful sixth year to cover for the Shemitah year would double prior to the Shemitah-Jubilee combination.

More complete information about Jubilee can be found in the book *Israel FIRST! The Key to Understanding the Blood Moons, Shemitah, Promises to Israel, and the Coming Jubilee.*

Agricultural field in Israel (Photo: Sherwood Burton)

Is the Jubilee currently being observed in Israel? No, and here is why.

First, there is no clear general agreement about when the Jubilee year actually happens. Of course we will discuss this more going forward as this is the mystery we all want to solve.

Second, unlike when the Land of Israel was settled thousands of years ago, there is no longer a clear understanding of the boundaries of tribal ownership. We currently do not have an exact method of knowing the borders of each tribe and, of course, are clueless as to the borders of family plots. In addition, barring a prophetic dictate, it would be nearly impossible for anyone to prove which tribe or family they descended from, so that their property could be returned.

Third, there is no tradition of Jubilee observance. The process of religious observance of festivals in Judaism is steeped in tradition. Changes do not come easily; they are deliberated and debated from all sides and we look to past sources of information passed down from the rabbis. But concerning the Jubilee we have no such records.

In fact, there seems to exist no clear evidence that the Jubilee was ever observed in the history of the Jewish people in the ancient land of Israel.

Therefore, to begin observance of the Jubilee would be a momentous undertaking. Nothing so important would ever be agreed to easily. However, the potential impact for celebrating the Jubilee could also be historic.

Some Rabbis, including Maimonides, believe that observance (or re-establishment of the observance) of the Jubilee could actually be a sign of the arrival of the Messianic age!

So it is significant to see early signs in Israel of a renewed interest in the Shemitah and now the Jubilee. It is even more significant to me because we might be in the midst of a Jubilee year right now!

What is the big idea behind Jubilee? Why is it so important?

The Jubilee is about freedom! The Torah's explicit statement to proclaim freedom is even enshrined on the Liberty Bell with the words: "Proclaim liberty throughout the land unto all the inhabitants thereof."

Liberty Bell

Among Americans, this ranks among the most treasured quotes from the Bible (Leviticus 25:10), and represents all the striving for freedom and liberty that the United States was built upon. The forms that freedom took in biblical times may have been different from the way it manifests in modern times, but the basic idea is the same. Slaves were freed regardless of the reason or term of their slavery. Land purchases were all temporary — the land really belonged to God. The land itself was freed from its task of producing food.

Nowadays, we may look to different forms that freedom may take. We might emphasize freedom of speech or religion or some other human endeavor. We may see it as a quest of individual freedoms over the power of the government. It may take the form of freedom from oppression or hatred or control. But whatever form freedom takes, it is arguably the state of human society that is treasured above all others. Elsewhere in this book, I write about Jonathan Pollard being released in the U.S. and suggest this might be a sign of the Jubilee. And in December 2015, another reputed Israeli spy, Ouda Tarabin, was released by Egypt. Some observers assign significance of Jubilee proportions to the release of Meir Ettinger, an Israeli Jew held for over a year by Israeli authorities.

That the biblical calendar celebrates freedom through the restarting of the Jubilee cycle is only fitting. The Bible has brought a great measure of freedom to the world through its wisdom, its insight into human nature, and its great revelation of one God who creates, sustains, and guides the universe. Is there any better way to usher in the next great cycle in the calendar than to "proclaim liberty throughout the land"?

Can we bring this half-century celebration of freedom back into our lives? This is not a question for the Jews alone, but for all those who treasure the Bible and look to it for spiritual sustenance.

Perhaps the time has come to revive this long-forgotten observance. Maybe those Jubilee years, coming as rarely as they do, signify something more than a few technical laws from the Old Testament. Maybe they represent something greater than that, the significance of which will only be understood as the decades and centuries and Jubilees role by. Only God knows — and only the future will tell.

Stefa Niyah

It would be awesome to restore the Torah by observing the jubilee years again. I'm not sure but don't Karaites observe this commandment? I´m going to Israel in about a month and I would like to get in touch with farmers, asking whether they observe the agricultural restrictions. I hope I will have success by finding a trusting farmer where I can buy my food in order to live my life according to YHWHs will! What is your opinion on this? Is there anybody who would also like to restore this important commandment again?

Frederick Ball

I think the smittah years therefore Jubilee are lost to us. That when Moshiach comes, That will be the Jubilee, either He knows the count, or since He is King, it won't matter whenever He comes it will be Jubilee.

Elijah comes preceding Moshiach, to restore all things. So who's talked to Elijah?

Laurence Bosma

INCREDIBLY AMAZING, we have the 120th Jubilee from creation, the 70th from Joshua crossing the Jordan, the 49th from the time of Ezra, also Rabbi Judah Ben Samuel's 11th jubilee and the 3rd Jubilee from the Balfour declaration with 1967 and the 6 day war being during the 2nd making 2016 the next Jubilee!

See the links: The 120th Jubilee year since creation will be 2016: http://yahuwah-is.net/Files/ScripturesEndTimes.html

Divine Dilemma

We have concluded the introduction to the Jubilee. After our invitation to jump into a mystery detective story, we have now looked at the Jubilee from the following perspectives:

- Israeli (1967 and the Six-Day War)

- Catholic

- Secular

- Protestant

- Jewish

We are now ready to talk about the Hebrew calendar, and why the year 1917 reveals a divine dilemma regarding the Jubilee.

Many people see the 1967 Six-Day War and reunification of Jerusalem as such important events that they might be a signal from God that a Jubilee occurred that year. When we count 49 or 50 years from 1967 we get to either 2016 or 2017, which means that these years could be critical as well.

In the comments, two questions have been asked multiple times.

- Why are you talking about 2016 and 2017 instead of the Hebrew calendar years?

- Aren't you going to talk about the Balfour Declaration in 1917, etc?

We have every intention of discussing these items, but first we wanted to establish the foundation of the Jubilee. With that accomplished, let us look into each of these excellent and appropriate questions in turn, to reveal a divine dilemma!

The Hebrew (Jewish) calendar begins on Rosh Hashanah (literally "head of the year") and is the first day of the month of Tishri, noted in the Bible as the Feast of Trumpets. The most recent Jewish Year, 5776 (that is, 5,776 years since the Creation), began at sundown September 13, 2015, and will last until sundown October 2, 2016. This Jewish calendar has been kept faithfully by Jews for over 2000 years, at least back to the period of the Second Temple. Included in the continuous tracking were the identification of the Sabbath Rest Years, or Shemitah years, even while the Jews were exiled after 70 AD.

In 325 AD, at the Council of Nicea, Constantine forcefully separated the Christian calendar (including Easter) from direct alignment with the Jewish calendar. The Shemitah years were ignored, and the Jews were able to continue to track their own seven-year Shemitah cycles without interference from Christians. Today, although there are exceptions, most Christians look to the Jewish tracking of the Shemitah years for their identification. That is what Jonathan Cahn did in his book, *The Mystery of the Shemitah*. In fact, he went beyond simply accepting the Jewish tracking of seven-year cycles; he showed how the Jewish tracking actually correlated with the economic cycles of the United States. The message is that the Shemitah year is alive and well, and is still used by God as a clock to govern the world's financial systems.

However, as faithful as the Jewish tracking of the seven-year cycles has been over the last 2,000 years or more, Jews have not agreed on historical identification of when Jubilee years might have occurred. There is even Jewish debate about whether they occur every 49 years or every 50 years.

This lack of a defined Jewish Jubilee calendar is for our purposes a huge opportunity! If Jews and Christians come together in the examination of the facts around this mystery, together we might be able to solve this mystery. What an opportunity we have to do some interesting work together! The Shemitah is already decided. Not only have the Jews been tracking it for centuries, but God seems to have weighed in and confirmed those cycles through the financial cycles of the U.S. and the Western world. For more information, refer to the Shemitah section of our book, *Israel FIRST!*

The big question before us in this series, therefore, is whether God will also weigh in on the Jubilee cycles by orchestrating real-world events that would give us clues about when this amazing year might occur.

This brings us to the pivotal year of 1917, because God did allow two things to happen in 1917 that still have people talking 99 years later.

First, on November 2, 1917, the British Cabinet issued the Balfour Declaration promising the best endeavors of the British government toward the establishment of a homeland for the Jews. In other words, it was a promise to help the Jews return to their property and to their families!

Lord Balfour and the Balfour Declaration (Photo: Wikicommons)

Second, just five weeks later, on December 11, 1917, the British army under General Allenby succeeded in capturing Jerusalem from the Ottoman Turks, who had held it for 400 years. General Allenby dismounted from horseback and humbly entered the Jerusalem through the Jaffa Gate. With the capture of not only Jerusalem but all of Palestine, the British Army now had the means by which to fulfill the very promise it had made five weeks earlier!

General Allenby enters Jerusalem
(Photo: British Government Archives)

So, the year 1917 is considered almost as important a year in Jewish history as 1967, which beheld the reunification of Jerusalem.

The years 1917 and 1967 years are 50 years apart. Therefore we must be open to look for what God might do in 2017.

But wait! This simple math misses something. What happens if we look at those two dates from the standpoint of the Jewish Calendar?

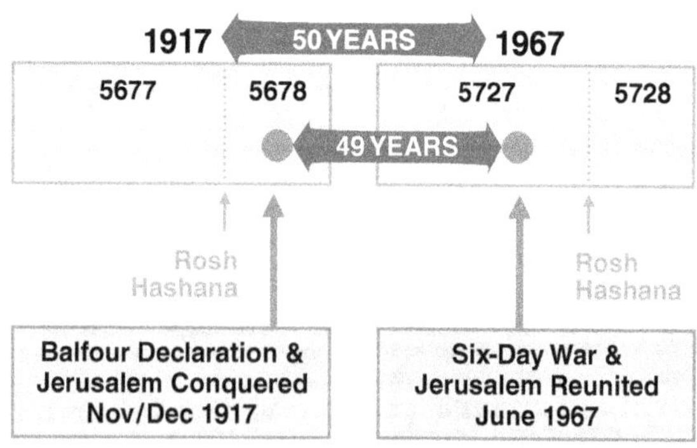

(Chart: Bob O'Dell)

1917 and 1967 are 50 years apart, but when looking at the dates from the perspective of the Jewish calendar, they are only 49 Jewish years apart. In 1917, the key events occurred late, in the Jewish year 5678, whereas in 1967 they occurred earlier, in the Jewish year 5727.

This is a divine dilemma! Our current situation allows those who hold the 50-year Gregorian calendar theory and the 49-year Jewish calendar theory to be equally satisfied. It is almost like God wants both camps of thought to be equally drawn into this search for the Jubilee.

However, it is hard to imagine how both camps can be satisfied this time. A 49 year pattern and a 50-year pattern must diverge from each other in the coming Jubilee. We would expect a clear winner to emerge.

If the 49 Jewish year theory is correct, and God confirms the Jubilee Year pattern through world events, then WE WILL SEE SOMETHING IMPORTANT BETWEEN NOW AND OCTOBER 2, 2016.

If the 50-year theory is correct, and God confirms the Jubilee pattern through world events, then WE WILL SEE SOMETHING IMPORTANT BETWEEN JANUARY 1, 2017 AND DECEMBER 31, 2017.

Questions for discussion and thought

What do *you* say? Do you already have a strongly-held opinion on which is correct: the 49-year theory or the 50-year theory? Why or why not?

Jaap Dieleman

I was puzzling myself for a while about the 49 and 50 years. Personality I believe the 50th year is the First year of the next cycle, Just like the last high 'Do' in an octave is the 8th Note of that octave, and at the same the First Note of the next Octave. Besides 8 stands For a NEW beginning. I am anxious To hear what others have found regarding this mystery

CHAPTER 7

Judah ben Samuel

In the last chapter, we showed that the years 1917 and 1967 and the amazing events that occurred in them can justify both a 50-year cycle between Jubilees and a 49-year cycle. We called this a divine dilemma, knowing that the events of 2016 and 2017 have the potential to reveal which is correct. The initial comments we have received have been excellent and are split between preference for a 49-year interval and 50-year interval between Jubilees. That chapter concluded our introduction to the Jubilee.

We now begin a two-part discussion about a Jubilee prophecy making the rounds on the Internet for the last eight years that has been attributed to Judah ben Samuel, known in Jewish circles as Yehudah Hachassid.

In this chapter we will bring you up to date on that Internet prophecy, and in the next chapter we will tell you about our fascinating visit to the headquarters of *Israel Today* magazine. *Israel Today* published the first article on this prophecy in 2008, and we will reveal brand-new information about this topic.

First of all, who is Judah ben Samuel?

Judah ben Samuel (Rabbi Yehudah Hachassid) was born in Speyer, Germany, and died in Regensburg, Germany, in 1217. His date of birth is omitted in the Jewish Encyclopedia but was probably 1140 or 1150. He certainly lived during the time of the Crusades and was aware of the state of Jerusalem. He was considered one of the fathers of a certain kind of Jewish mysticism (Chassidei Ashkenaz) that emphasized moral ethics and prayer. Around 1195 he settled in Regensburg and it was here that he wrote an important work, *Sefer Hasidim* (Book of the Pious). This seminal work deals with many matters, including pride, prayer, reward and punishment, penitence, Sabbath, fasting, and more.

It is said that Rabbi ben Samuel wrote or at least contributed to a *Sefer Gematriyot* (Book on Numerology) and a *Sefer Hakavod* (Book of Glory), but unfortunately our efforts could not locate either of these works. They may have been lost. Should anyone reading this have access to either of them, you have something that belongs in a Jewish history museum.

Judah ben Samuel's writings are difficult to follow, as they are mostly a collection of loosely connected thoughts rather than organized systematically with overall thematic statements. A *Jewish Encyclopedia* article on him written in 1899 concludes like this:

[Historical scholar Leopold] *Zunz says of him: "To vindicate whatever is noble in human endeavors, and the highest aspirations of the Israelite, and to discover the inmost truths alluded to in the Sacred Books, seemed to be the ultimate purpose of a mind in which poetic, moral, and divine qualities were fused."*

He was well respected in his day, and is even today. He was certainly an influence on the Vilna Gaon, recognized as one of the greatest scholars in Jewish history. Ben Shmuel had mystical leanings, and according to his students he had a burning desire to see the coming of the Messiah.

Now, we fast forward to the Internet Age and describe the Jubilee prophecy that has begun to be attributed to him in thousands of web pages and writings since 2008.

The Internet Prophecy

The prophecy attributed to Judah ben Samuel goes like this:

When the Ottomans conquer Jerusalem, they will rule over Jerusalem for eight Jubilees. Afterwards, Jerusalem will become no-man's land for one Jubilee, and then in the ninth Jubilee it will once again come back into the possession of the Jewish nation — which would signify the beginning of the Messianic end time.

After Judah ben Samuel's death in 1217, it was actually the Mamluks who would capture Jerusalem first. They did so in 1250. But the Ottomans would take Jerusalem in 1517 and they would hold it for exactly 400 years until 1917, as we discussed in the previous chapter.

The articles that promote this prophecy point out that 400 years between 1517 and 1917 is eight Jubilee periods exactly, assuming that the Jubilee is 50 years in length. They further note that 1917 to 1967 is the ninth Jubilee period, during which Jerusalem was controlled by the British and then divided between Israel and Jordan between 1948 and 1967.

Old City walls built by the Ottomans. The road pictured marks part of the 1949 "green line" that divided East and West Jerusalem until 1967. (Photo: Sherwood Burton)

Many of these articles then go further and make an inference that by the tenth Jubilee, the Messiah should return, i.e., by 2017. This is a stretch, because even the original prophecy wording makes no such claim.

The writers of this book also make no such claim, although we would gladly welcome the Messiah at any time. In fact, Bob observes that according to this prophecy, the case could be made for placing the commencement of the Messianic age immediately in 1967, which he sees as similar to the claim that Christians make when they say the "times of the Gentiles" were over as of 1967, according to Luke 21:24:

Jerusalem would be trampled under foot by the Gentiles until the times of the Gentiles are fulfilled.

Finally, many of the Internet articles also point out that the time between Judah Ben Samuel's death in 1217 to the conquering of Jerusalem by the Ottomans in 1517 is exactly 300 years, which itself is six Jubilee periods.

In summary, this prophecy seems to make a strong *historical pattern argument* for a 50-year Jubilee cycle, because it shows a long-term sequence of historical events occurring in a repeating 50-year pattern over hundreds of years.

The Problems

The Internet prophecy as written above and attributed to Judah ben Samuel, however, has three big problems.

First, a number of Internet articles sceptical of this prophecy have pointed out that the Ottoman empire mentioned in the prophecy did not even begin until 1299, more than 80 years after his death. The term "Ottoman" comes from the man, Osman I, who was not born until 40 years after Judah ben Samuel's death. More generally, the "Turks" were segmented, scattered and in continuous decline at the time Judah ben Samuel lived. This begs the question of *exactly how is the original prophecy worded in its original language and context?* That question leads us to a bigger problem.

Second, the available works of Judah ben Samuel do not contain any reference to this prophecy as far as we are aware. Had there been such reference, it would certainly have garnered the attention of Jews given the respect paid to him.

Third, the announcement of this prophecy was not made until a few years ago, essentially after most or all of its events were completed. Predictions that are released after-the-fact immediately raise concerns.

It was these problems that caused us to discover that there is exactly one original source for everything written on the subject. This prophecy comes from an article published in Israel Today magazine, March 2008, page 18, by Ludwig Schneider. We immediately contacted the article's author requesting information about the source of the prophecy, but have received no reply as of the time of this writing.

In the next chapter, we will tell you about our fascinating meeting with Ludwig Schneider's son, Aviel Schneider, the editor-in-chief of *Israel Today* magazine. We will share what he told us about the article, his father, and the source of the prophecy.

Questions for discussion and thought

Does anyone know of other historical arguments for a "50-year pattern between Jubilees" that are as strong as the prophecy described in this chapter?

Guido Galo Grunauer

"count me in."

There are many written in the Holy Bible that are full of prophecies to be fulfilled according to the times for the second coming of the Messiah first cloud (rapture of the church) and after the great tribulation with all his saints, at the end of the 144.000 sealed people brought back to the people of Israel to the truth and the rest of the world becomes the father This is what judgment call nations spoken of in Daniel, Malachi, EZEKIEL, REVELATION whose word will be fulfilled, waiting the construction of the third temple and desolate appearance of the wicked son of iniquity.

Marilyn Kline

Because of the 4 blood moons over 2 years on Jewish Feast Days, something big is going to happen! I believe it will be the Antichrist will show up, amid some other big events. The War of Gog and Magog hasn't happened yet (Ezekiel 38 and 39). Russia and Persia are already in place for it, above Israel in Syria. Israel has a huge natural gas field and now an oil field has been discovered close to the borrder with Syria! Russia's prime exports are gas and oil, besides armaments. Friction there.

Since Israel was attacked, the world will feel shame once again, and I believe allow her to build the Third Temple and resume sacrifices. In the Gog u'Magog War, God's opening salvo is a huge earthquake where walls will fall down, so perhaps the Temple Mount will be clear of what is on it now. Since Yahshua will call for us with the blast of a Trumpet, many of us always look to Rosh Hashanah, the Feast of Trumpets, as a likely day for our bridegroom to come for us, as in a Jewish custom of coming for his bride in the middle of the night. The bride knows the house he is building is almost finished, so she will be alert and ready. Yahshua's believers are called "The Bride of Christ". Seeing it acted out is a beautiful sight (Zola Levitt Ministries)!

Rabbis seem to think Messiah is coming this year, but I think they will be tricked by Antichrist, who WILL be performing miracles (the Bible says they will be false miracles). Messiah will not return until the 7 years of Tribulation are at their END, at the last battle, at Armageddon, where he will slay the 200 million soldiers coming against Jerusalem. He will plant His feet on the Mt. of Olives, where he ascended to heaven from 2,000 years ago.

Ronda Carifelle Longard

How is it that the term Jubilee was lost at all? If Passover was observed for millenia now, then why is the Jubilee not?

Phil Gram

I believe the Rabbi was onto something. That said another rabbi was also on to something. What the first rabbi and the second rabbi knew was that things must be perfect in timing and then and only then will Messiah come. Until then Hashem has the date firmly in His mind and He's not saying, but the first rabbi said to expect it when you least expect it.

Hector Zuniga

Pray that won't happen in winter time, but any way come Mashiach of Yisrael, even if You tarry I will keep waiting for You.

Lorio Moten

Shalom ISRAEL . The JUBILEE has started.

CHAPTER 8

Prophetic Memories

In the last chapter, we introduced a Jubilee prophecy attributed to Judah ben Samuel, also known by Jews as Yehudah Hachassid, that has spread like wildfire over the Internet in the last few years. In that chapter we promised that we would disclose new information about the source.

That new information comes from a meeting that Gidon Ariel and Bob O'Dell had with Aviel Schneider, editor-in-chief of *Israel Today* magazine, whose father, Ludwig Schneider, authored the original article about the prophecy in their March 2008 issue. It was from that one article that every other article originated.

Later in this chapter, I, Bob, will tell you what about this whole situation troubles me the most. But before that, let me start by quoting the exact words of Ludwig Schneider in introducing this prophecy to the world. Ludwig wrote about Judah ben Samuel on page 18 in the March 2008 issue of *Israel Today*:

> Before he died in the year 1217, he prophesied that the Ottoman Turks would conquer Jerusalem and rule the Holy City for "eight Jubilee years." A biblical jubilee year consists of 50 years. Fifty multiplied by eight equals 400 years.

> Afterwards, according to ben Samuel, the Ottomans would be driven out of Jerusalem, which would remain no-man's land for one jubilee year. In the tenth jubilee year, Jerusalem would return to the Jewish people and then the Messianic end times would begin.

> This came to pass 300 years after his death. He could not have based his prophecy on events that could be foreseen, but only on

the results of his study of the Bible.

Later in that article, Ludwig Schneider wrote the words that would cause this story to take on a life of its own over the next eight years:

According to this timeline, it is possible that 2017 or 2018 will be a decisive year for Israel because it will be 70 years after 1947, the UN decision for the establishment of Israel, and 50 years after the reunification of Jerusalem.

Ludwig closed out his article with the statement:

We don't know the day or the hour of his coming, but we are not talking about the return of Jesus. We are talking about God's timetable for Israel.

After we found this article and could find no earlier source material anywhere regarding this prophecy, Gidon contacted the offices of *Israel Today* asking for the best way for us to connect with Ludwig. The office suggested we send an email that would be forwarded to him. We wrote, asking for any additional information he might be willing to disclose about the original source of the prophecy. We got a confirmation that the email had been forwarded to him, and then waited about 10 days for a reply. At this point I phoned Aviel Schneider, his son, asking for his help. Aviel told me not to expect an answer from Ludwig, but agreed to meet Gidon and me face-to-face at the magazine's Jerusalem offices to hear our request for detailed sources.

He began by expressing his frustration, saying, "For seven years nobody talked to us about this issue, until a few months ago." We were stunned to hear this, given that Google finds more than 60,000 web pages on the topic.

Aviel confirmed that the March 2008 article is the only occasion that his father ever wrote on the topic of this prophecy.

Asked about the source of the prophecy, Aviel told us that his father had a large collection of Jewish writings in the German language. Aviel believes the source material for the prophecy came from that library.

Had Aviel ever seen the specific prophecy himself? No.

I then asked the main question we had come to ask, "Would Aviel be willing to ask his father to locate the book in which this prophecy was written?" To my question Aviel responded in Hebrew to Gidon. Gidon, turned to me and translated in English: "I asked my father to find it and he said 'With so many books, I wouldn't know where it is.'"

Indeed, while Ludwig Schneider has an exceedingly sharp mind (he still writes regularly for Israel Today), he is elderly and eight years ago is a long time. Furthermore, we can all understand and appreciate the decision of a son to guard his elderly father from those whose questions would now undoubtedly raise stress. "I take care that he is protected," Aviel told us.

Actually, the stakes are higher than our research of the Jubilee. The important point is that we can find no record of this prophecy being discussed by Jews before 2008. The Jewish people value and respect the writings of their sages. They would receive with great gratitude any newly discovered writings from one of their greatest sages, particularly after the destruction of so many books by Nazi Germany in the Holocaust. Clearly there are no opposing Jewish motives here: prophetic statements from Jewish sages are pronounced occasionally, so that breaks no new ground. This Jewish prophecy, if confirmed, would bring nothing but honor to the Jewish people and Judah ben Samuel — *if* he wrote it, that is.

Please understand that in calling this into question, I make no accusation of Ludwig Schneider! And neither is there any danger that this article will ever reach him, according to his son. Ludwig has written positively about Israel for over 40 years and this should command tremendous respect. Let us all follow the wishes of his son and let him live in peace.

But, I can speak from personal experience about how easy it is to get one's facts or dates mixed when looking at old source material. I once wrote an article that used old Dutch sources to offer new insights about the activities of the Dutch Reformed church in Indonesia in the early 1800s. However, and this is the key point, *because I disclosed my sources*, a Christian researcher was able to suggest that I double-check one of my source assumptions. To my dismay, he was absolutely correct, and I had to quickly put out a retraction and moderate my initial claims accordingly. It was humbling to say the least.

Yet, in the case of this Jubilee prophecy we are talking about a situation that is more complicated: an ancient prophecy possibly written in Middle High German that was never quoted verbatim, but only interpreted and translated into English. That interpretation then used the term "Ottoman Turks," which just doesn't make sense during the life of Yehuda ben Samuel. As we mentioned in the previous chapter, the Ottoman empire was founded by — and named for — a man who was not born until 40 years after Judah ben Samuel's death. In addition, the Turks were segmented and in continual decline during ben Samuel's life. So the need to look at the exact words used in ancient German, and to see them in their context is critical! In addition, books were rare and multiple authors often combined their writings into a single work, over a period of years, making authorship and dating less certain.

Having been given no permission to search for this quote ourselves, we concluded by asking Aviel if he might be willing to search his father's library for this prophecy. He told us, "Even if I found it, I might decide

Jerusalem in 1916, in the latter days of the Ottoman Empire (Photo: Wikicommons)

not to write about it," the result of his frustration with how past articles were propagated by the Christian media. He concluded with, "In this case, you are on your own. What we have written, we have written."

What does all this mean regarding this Jubilee series of articles? It means that the fact that Jerusalem was reunified in 1967 is reason enough to be watching events closely in 2016 and 2017 (49 and 50 years after that date). Such examination requires no further motivation.

And of this prophecy? Until someone discovers an ancient writing that contains the words "Jerusalem," "eight," and "Jubilee" in the same sentence of a larger work, and releases that work for examination, this prophecy must be regarded as hearsay. As much as Jews might desire to see more honor go to a pious Jewish man, and as much as Christians might desire a prophetic indication that some amazing event will happen regarding Israel or Jesus in the next year or two, we must all refrain from using this prophecy to bolster any such claims. It should not be propagated until the original sources are found.

What mistakes were made? In my opinion there were two mistakes, and the confusion we have on the Internet today is the result of *both* of them.

First, it would have been advisable for Ludwig Schneider to carefully document the source of the prophecy in his original article, including quoting the words in their original language, including even a photograph of the source, given that he was introducing ground-breaking research.

Second, and here is what troubles me the most: Aviel's statement that, "For *seven years* nobody talked to us about this issue." The main propagation of this prophecy began, as far as I can tell, in 2010 when a pastor postulated that the Great Tribulation should begin in 2010 in order that Jesus would return by 2017, according to Judah ben Samuel's prophecy. (Ludwig himself made no such claim.) The number of web pages, articles and videos then began to increase rapidly.

Why did nobody ask to see the original source material before now? It is true that many blog posts in the last few years have called the prophecy into question. Those negative blog posts should have created an even greater eagerness to request the source writings! Aviel Schneider, the editor of *Israel Today* did not turn away our request for a meeting. On the contrary, he received us quickly and obviously felt bad about the situation. Had anyone thought to ask for source material within the first couple of years, the story of this prophecy might not be in limbo.

We must take this case study as an exhortation to communicate with other Christians more than we do, even as Jesus prayed for us in John 17:21:

...that all of them may be one, Father, just as you are in me and I am in you. (NIV)

Again I don't blame anyone specifically here because to "connect" takes both parties to agree to do so—one is not enough.

But, on the positive side, I find it fascinating that our investigation into these sources came as a result of an evangelical Christian and an Orthodox Jew connecting, trying to find the truth behind the Jubilee. It was Gidon's checking on his side, and inability to find Jewish sources of the Judah ben Samuel prophecy that alerted us to go looking for the source. Without him, I would have assumed that the original Jewish writings had been known for centuries.

Perhaps the idea of Jew and Christian working together can be a model that bears good fruit in cases like this going forward. In the meantime, Gidon suggests that we all keep in mind one of the more famous quotes of Abraham Lincoln, who famously said, "Don't believe everything you read on the Internet!"

Lauren Walter Berns

Why do we need that prophecy we have two witnesses that include the "most overlooked" prophecy in the Tanakh/Bible:

'HEZEKIAH'S RETURNING 18 YEARS'

Why hasn't the "returning 18 year" prophecy of Hezekiah gotten the heightened time of awareness from Judaism or Christianity that it deserves while it is given 11 chapters of coverage in the books of 2 Chronicles, 2 Kings and Isaiah?

See http://www.fivedoves.com/letters/feb2016/lauren29.htm

Shalom and pray for the peace of Jerusalem.

Marilyn Kline

So, this is a Jubilee Year? The Blood Moons on Jewish Feast Days are completed. In the Middle was a total Solar Eclipse. Seems to me like God is screaming it from the skies!

Just remember, Jewish people, Yahshua is coming back for His Own before the 7 years of Tribulation. If the person shows up who the Bible terms "the Antichrist", please do NOT believe he is your Messiah. Even if he seems to perform miracles, do not believe he is the Messiah. You will sign a 7-year Peace Treaty with this man (who has no interest in women, it says), and he will break that treaty half-way through it!

CHAPTER 9

One, Two, Fifty

Before we continue, it is clear from the comments that something we were attempting to explain about the "divine dilemma" is still a bit confusing. So let us now apologize for that confusion, and clarify it.

We have said that one of the Mysteries of the Lost Jubilee is whether Jubilees repeat every 49 or every 50 years. The very idea that Jubilees might repeat every 49 years seems to make no logical sense to some people because of what Leviticus 25:10 clearly says:

*You shall thus consecrate the **fiftieth** year and proclaim a release through the land to all its inhabitants. It shall be a jubilee for you, and each of you shall return to his own property, and each of you shall return to his family.* (emphasis added)

So let us explain how Jubilees could potentially repeat every 49 years. The issue revolves around what year you start your counting to that fiftieth year. We will explain it like this:

Let's imagine a new community that is formed in complete isolation from the rest of the world, with only the book of Leviticus in its possession. The people decide to follow the teachings of Leviticus 25 and start to count the years. They start this counting in the very first year that their community formed. They call that founding year "Year One." Every time a new year begins, they count it as a new year. They get to the seventh year, and they call that their first Sabbatical year — which is the year that they let the land rest. They count the next year to be year eight, and they count year 14 as their second Sabbatical year. They keep counting and they get to year 49, the seventh Sabbatical year, and celebrate it as a year of rest. Then the next year, the fiftieth year, is the year of the Jubilee, which (according to Leviticus) is another Sabbatical year, but also has other special celebrations associated with it. This Jubilee year is brand new, not only because of its uniqueness, but also because nobody has ever celebrated two back-to-back years of rest in the community's history.

As the story continues, and since 50 years is a long time, all but the youngest of the original leaders of the community have died. New leaders are in place. As the new leaders look at Leviticus, two opinions arise about how to continue this pattern. The question boils down to what year should become the next "Year One" to start counting to the next Jubilee?

Two camps emerge. One camp, we'll call them the 49ers, say that the Jubilee year is not only a year of celebration, but it is "Year One" of the counting to the next Jubilee. The 49ers say that this interpretation is the best because it keeps the Sabbatical years happening every seven years without any interruptions. They point to the words of Leviticus 25:8:

You are also to count off seven Sabbaths of years for yourself, seven times seven years, so that you have the time of the seven Sabbaths, namely forty-nine years.

They see a strong emphasis on the repeating seven-year cycles over and over, the emphasis on 49 years in the cycle.

But another camp arises, let's call them the 50ers. They believe that the counting to the next Jubilee year should only start *after* the Jubilee ends. They want to see the Jubilees occur every 50 years, because two Jubilees makes a clean century. The community can celebrate its one hundredth anniversary during Jubilee. The 50ers also say that the Jubilee is so important that it should not be shared with any other year or be counted for any other purpose. "The Jubilee year should stand on its own," they say.

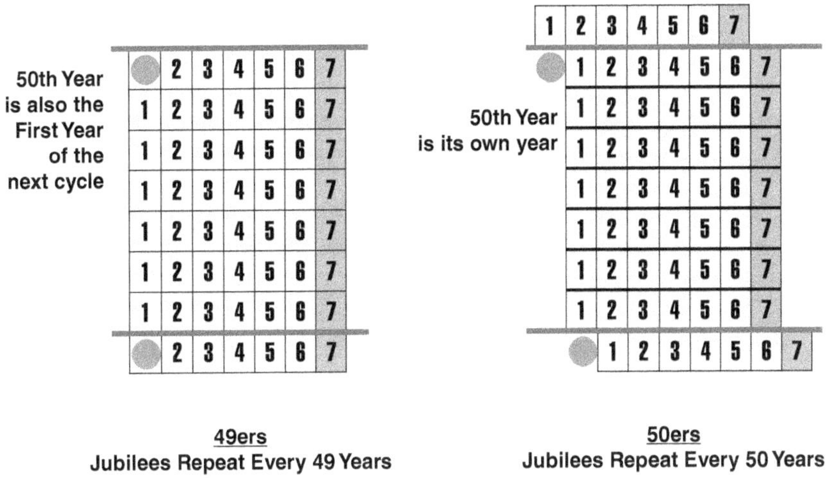

49ers — 50th Year is also the First Year of the next cycle

●	2	3	4	5	6	7
1	2	3	4	5	6	7
1	2	3	4	5	6	7
1	2	3	4	5	6	7
1	2	3	4	5	6	7
1	2	3	4	5	6	7
1	2	3	4	5	6	7
●	2	3	4	5	6	7

49ers
Jubilees Repeat Every 49 Years

50ers — 50th Year is its own year

1	2	3	4	5	6	7
●	1	2	3	4	5	6	7
1	2	3	4	5	6	7
1	2	3	4	5	6	7
1	2	3	4	5	6	7
1	2	3	4	5	6	7
1	2	3	4	5	6	7
1	2	3	4	5	6	7
●	1	2	3	4	5	6	7

50ers
Jubilees Repeat Every 50 Years

(Chart: Bob O'Dell)

In the meeting between the two camps, the 49ers say, "It is critical that the seven-year cycles continue in regular intervals. Your method is too complex because it restarts the calendar every 50 years. Would you tell us that the days of the week should be interrupted every seven weeks, and would you create a brand-new day to be inserted between Saturday and Sunday? That is extremely confusing." Then the 50ers respond and say, "Our method keeps track of the centuries automatically. And besides, your idea also has problems, because by calling the Jubilee a 'Year One' it means that every 49 years, the farmers have a 'short stretch' when they only work the land for five years, not six. Your method makes it harder on them to prepare for the Sabbath year."

Traditionally the church is solidly in the 50ers camp. The Catholic Church has even gone further and started their first Jubilee in the year 1300 to make it fit nicely on century boundaries. Then, in the past 100 years, they began to allow 'extra-ordinary' years of Jubilee (they just happen to have called one for 2016).

One of the strongest voices on this topic, at least by number of books sold, is Jonathan Cahn's. Cahn is solidly in the 49ers camp, because he sees the Balfour declaration and Six-Day War as occurring 49 years apart, both on the year *after* a Sabbatical (Shemitah) year ended. By the way, he calls the Jubilee a "Super-Shemitah" since it is a Sabbath rest year that occurs after seven seven-year cycles.

The Orthodox Jewish world has been counting the Sabbatical years for over 2,000 years and has never inserted Jubilee years. This repeating cycle has been correlated to significant world events, as has been popularized by the books by Jonathan Cahn. If Jubilee years were inserted, as the 50ers suggest, the correlation no longer works! This leads some to consider that the 49ers camp is correct.

But the situation is more complex because, while Orthodox Jews counted Sabbatical years during the exile, they were knowingly not counting Jubilee years, since there was no way to fulfill the commandments of the Jubilee outside of the land of Israel. In fact, there is a difference of opinion between Orthodox rabbis about whether the 49ers or 50ers camp is more correct. Until the first Jubilee is declared, however, this can remain unresolved for them. We have interesting new information to reveal on this topic later on in this book!

The main purpose of this chapter is to highlight that both the 49ers camp and the 50ers camps have merit. Reasonable people who love the Scriptures can come to different conclusions about whether Jubilees ought to be repeating every 49 years or every 50 years. We, Gidon and Bob, reveal an opinion in Bonus Chapter at the end of this book, and give our reasons. But we are willing to hold our conclusions loosely and to be wrong. In fact, the most exciting prospect in front of us, is to see whether God may show us His thoughts on the matter through world events.

We have grounded this book on the amazing events of November/ December 1917 and June 1967, which were 49 ½ years apart. Using the standard Gregorian calendar, those events seem to be 50 years apart which satisfies the 50ers, yet on the Hebrew calendar they fall 49 years apart which satisfies the 49ers! Based on that pattern:

- If something amazing happens to Israel between now and October 2, 2016, the end of the current Jewish year, then the 49ers could claim a sequence of three important events with Jubilees repeating every 49 years.

- If something amazing happens between January 1, 2017 and December 31, 2017, then the 50ers could claim a sequence of three important events with Jubilees repeating every 50 years.

- There are a few other combinations possible, as have been mentioned by readers, such as something happening between October 3, 2016, and December 31, 2016, or if amazing events happen in both 2016 and 2017! We may deal with those too in the future.

But, there is a very different way to examine this pattern. Rather than speculate about what God might do this year, we could look backward!

Questions for discussion and thought

God honors our willingness to respect an alternate view, and to hold our own opinions loosely enough to be willing to be wrong. Would you like to share a story of "respect" or "holding loosely" and what happened over time when your view was either confirmed or changed by later facts?

Theresa Palmer

Changed and confirmed, since I am not a serious student...learning.

Daryl Jubenville

Love the debates ! And interestingly they come to me at an interesting time in my life.

I am CHRISTIAN and in the past few months I've discovered the video teachings of Christian Rabbi Jonathan Cahn & a website called Israel 365 with Rabbi Tuly Weisz.

D'rea Daniel

This is a wonderful perspective...

Chesterfield Walrond

Daryl has said it correctly .the Hebrew calendar is God given therefore in Leviticus it say 50th year not 49th is the jubilee. After the 50th year you start the cycle over again . this is simple. Do you think that man know better than God. He says , my ways are not your ways ,neither are my thoughts yours.

The Jewish leaders has always has a problem with "obeying God" look at their history and God call them "rebels". The modern day leaders are the same. Joshua was told to drive out the people in the land no, they began to intermingle. Why was Jerusalem left in the hands of the Arabs after it was conquered. Disobedience has cause what Israel is facing.They always think they know better than God. So they will have to learn the hard way in the coming Jacob's troubles. Joel's prophecy will be fulfilled then.

Dennis Wright

Because of the events that coincide with the seven year cycle I have wondered if the Jubilee 50th year is in fact the first year of the next 49 year cycle. My belief is that something will happen this year and my tip is about 9th Av (or August 13). I don't only base this on Biblical prophecies but on predictions from others such as Nostradamus who predicted resurrection at the time of an Olympic Games and St. Malachy who claimed that the current Pope is the last one before the final redemption. It is certain that little time remains and our daily headlines showing "every hand against Israel" and the persecution of Christians and Jews in the "last days" as predicted in the Bible are a sure indication that the time is nigh.

D'rea Daniel

As I read this Holy Spirit brought to mind...."The Hidden Day"....

Marilyn Kline

I have read the Rabbi Jonathan Cahn's books. This week he is the featured guest speaker on Kenneth Copeland's Believer's Voice of Victory program on TBN (and probably other stations, too). I have gone ahead and watched all of this week's programs, and last week featured Cahn, too! Very lively discussions and Harbingers talked about!! So glad Kenneth Copeland had Cahn on!

In my heart I believe this is a Jubilee year, because the Jews got Jerusalem back in 1967, so surely, if anything was a Jubilee Year, getting Jerusalem back would be one!!

I look forward to this series. Very timely, since this is probably a Jubilee Year!!

CHAPTER 10

The Back Fifty

In the previous chapter, we explained an area of disagreement, from both history and Scripture, about whether Jubilees should repeat every 49 years or every 50 years. All this stems from the amazing capture of Jerusalem in December 1917 and the reunification of Jerusalem in June 1967, which were 49 ½ years apart. Those events are 50 years apart on the Gregorian calendar, and 49 years apart on the Jewish calendar!

Now we will go back in time and look 49 and 50 years prior to December 1917, to the year of 1868, and see what can be learned from history. Has God given us any clues about the Jubilee pattern?

Looking back 49 years, according to the Jewish calendar, the seven year Shemitah cycle began in fall of 1861 and lasted through fall of 1868. That means the Shemitah year occurred from the fall of 1867 to the fall of 1868, allowing for a Jubilee year potentially from the fall of 1868 to the fall of 1869. Did anything remarkable happened that year?

First, what should we be looking for? In principle we should be looking for freedom from slavery as well as property restored to the Jewish people. Did anything happen along those lines? *Yes.*

Germany had been in the process of bringing equality to its Jewish citizens in prior years, and it completed the process on December 3, 1868, when Saxony became the last region of its state to grant equality to all the Jews. Then later in that same year, Prussia, which controlled the region between Germany and Russia, created a confederation with Germany, thus creating even more widespread equality for the Jews on July 3, 1869. (For more information see Wikipedia's "History of Jews in Germany")

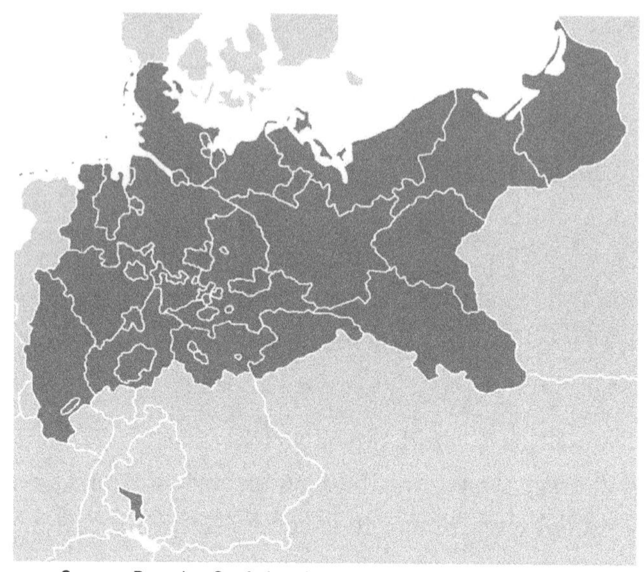

German-Prussian Confederation, 1869 (Source: Wikicommons)

This was a pivotal event in the emancipation of Jews in Europe. However, to be fair, we should point out that the Jewish emancipation in Europe is generally not dated until two years later in 1871, after the Franco-Prussian war brought into the Confederation more territory of what is now France, and the new southern states including Bavaria were added to the Confederation and forced to adopt Jewish equality. Nevertheless, the case can be reasonably made that the confederation of 1869 was the key decision, and that the events in 1871 were an expansion of territory of an empire that was being blessed by God for its positive stance towards the Jewish people. Indeed, we must note that the decision to grant full Jewish equality in all matters, including property rights, was born out of liberalism and an Enlightenment mentality that was often secular and anti-God. How ironic it is that it took a secular humanist movement to finally do what the church had not done in prior centuries in the very same region. Jewish freedom in

Germany would in fact last for 64 years, until the reign of Adolf Hitler began in 1933.

Interestingly, 1869 would also be the year that the Temple Society of Germany, referred to as the Templers — a sect of German Lutherans, would migrate to Palestine and set up communities in Haifa and on Jerusalem Road in Jaffa, on their way to establishing a small neighborhood in Jerusalem a few years later. With regard to Jerusalem itself, beginning in 1860, Jewish neighborhoods began to spring up outside the city walls in 1860, 1868, 1869, 1872, 1873 and 1874. We mention this because with regard to past Jubilee dates we have always connected those dates to Jerusalem as well.

Nahalat Shiv'a neighborhood, Jerusalem, founded 1869 (Source: Wikicommons)

Shifting our focus over to the Americas in that same key time period of fall 1868 to fall 1869, it is interesting to note that on December 25,

1868, the United States pardoned the last of the Confederate rebels. Confederate soldiers had been pardoned in phases over the preceding years since 1865, but the job was finally completed on December 25, 1869, allowing them full freedom to return to their homes and their families. This kind of action is very consistent with the principles behind the Jubilee.

But if the Jubilee is about the freeing of slaves, not just soldiers, can we find any landmark events involving the freeing of slaves in that pivotal year? Actually we cannot! The key events for the freeing of American slaves came in earlier years in the following phases:

- January 1, 1863: The Emancipation Proclamation (third year of a Shemitah cycle)

- December 18, 1865: The declaration of adoption of the Thirteenth Amendment that abolished slavery (fifth year of a Shemitah cycle)

- July 9, 1868: The adoption of the Fourteenth Amendment that guaranteed due process for all those born on American soil and solidified equal protection for former slaves under the law (seventh year of a Shemitah cycle — the Shemitah year)

Have you ever noticed how often key legislation or decisions with major repercussions occurs in a Shemitah year? Take, for instance, the legalization of abortion in 1973 and the gay marriage ruling in 2015! In fact, it is ironic once again to realize that *it was the Fourteenth Amendment* that was used as legal justification by the United States Supreme Court for the abortion and gay marriage rulings! In our book *Israel FIRST!*, we discuss the Shemitah year extensively and offer a spiritual reason for this connection in time. But, with regard to the freeing of slaves and the fact that it did not fall on the Jubilee year, we would point out that the Shemitah year requirement to release debts also carried with it the release of indentured servants who were working for a property owner. In this context, the release of American slaves in a Shemitah year makes absolute sense!

Now let us go back 50 years from 1917, to 1867, to look for key events in that year.

With respect to Jewish emancipation, 1867 was the year that Austria-Hungary was formed, and the year that Jews were given equal rights in that confederation. This is a milestone, albeit not as huge as the German-Prussian confederation two years later. With regard to Templer activities in Palestine, 1867 was actually the first attempt, but an unsuccessful one, to settle near Tel Shimron in Northern Israel. We would categorize this evidence as existing, although weak to moderate in its impact.

When we go back another 50 years from 1867, to 1817, we do not find any particular events of note. Perhaps our readers will?

When we go back 49 years from 1868-1869 to fall 1819 to fall 1820, we find only two events of note. The first was an attempt to quell cries for Jewish emancipation. In Wuerzburg, Germany, pleas for the emancipation of Jews evoked riots against Jews there, which eventually spread to Denmark and Poland. The Carlsbad Decrees were put in place that reduced freedoms in order to "restore order," but eventually they had the opposite effect and the Jews would only be emancipated 49 years later. Secondly, the year 1819 marks the launching of the first American warship in the African Slave Patrol, designed to catch slave-trading ships off the coast of Africa. This effort resulted in only small progress, capturing just 100 ships over the next 42 years. Operations ceased with the onset of the American Civil War. We again consider both of these events as existing, but very weak evidence.

So let us summarize our findings. Looking at all these events, it is clear that if a pattern exists in history, it is a pattern of increasing clarity. For the 49-year case we have:

49-YEAR JUBILEE	STRENGTH OF HISTORICAL EVIDENCE
1819-1820	Very Weak
1868-1869	Moderate
1917-1918	Strong
1966-1967	Extremely Strong

In the 50-year case we have:

50-YEAR JUBILEE	STRENGTH OF HISTORICAL EVIDENCE
1817	None that we could find
1867	Weak-Moderate
1917	Strong
1967	Extremely Strong

From the tables above, a slight advantage goes to a 49 year repeating Jubilee pattern.

Questions for discussion and thought

What do you think? If you were previously leaning towards a 50-year pattern, based on the evidence presented in this article are you leaning more towards a 49-year pattern now?

Dianne Witzell

The summary charts make it appear that there is an intensifying trend that could be pointing to the culmination of prophecy, especially as it seems pretty obvious we are in the latter part of the last days. It would be interesting to repeat this examination backwards through time to see if any patterns emerge relative to the Shemitah, Jubilee, and holy tetrads, whereby four consecutive total lunar eclipses occur on Jewish holy days.

CHAPTER 11

The Sanhedrin

In our last chapter, we went backwards from 1917 and looked 49 and 50 years into the past to see if there was evidence for past Jubilee years in history. Now we will look at the Jubilee from the perspective of the Jewish Sanhedrin.

The Sanhedrin was an assembly or council in Jewish history that had from 23 to 71 men appointed in every city. Each Sanhedrin would hear cases and make decisions according to Jewish law. This system came from the commandments of the Torah, such as in Deuteronomy 1:15-16:

So I took the heads of your tribes, wise and experienced men, and appointed them heads over you, leaders of thousands and of hundreds, of fifties and of tens, and officers for your tribes. Then I charged your judges at that time, saying, "Hear the cases between your fellow countrymen, and judge righteously between a man and his fellow countryman, or the alien who is with him. You shall not show partiality in judgment; you shall hear the small and the great alike. You shall not fear man, for the commandment is God's."

The Sanhedrin certainly existed in the Second Temple period, being led by such rabbis as Gamaliel in the time of Jesus, and was ultimately disbanded in the city of Tiberias around 358 AD. Over the centuries, much discussion was held about how a Sanhedrin would ever be re-established, once disbanded. A few attempts were made to re-establish the Sanhedrin over the centuries, but none ever attained the level reached in 2004, when a group of rabbis met in Israel and, using the process that had been put forth by Maimonides, established a new Sanhedrin in the very location it was disbanded. This body is not recognized by Israeli courts, nor is it even recognized as an arbiter of Jewish religious law by a majority of religious Jews in Israel. (The practice of Jews in the exile was to seek advice, decisions, and blessing from one's local rabbi, and this method continues today.) However, this new Sanhedrin is growing, from its first ordained rabbi to over 250 rabbis across Israel today.

We see in this nascent Sanhedrin some good qualities, and believe it is slowly gaining respect in the Jewish community. We see in its behavior a circumspect manner that looks for ways to be of help, rather than simply looking for ways to exercise and accrue authority. While Sanhedrin's rabbis boldly address issues that have lain dormant throughout the centuries of exile, they also realize their limits, and do not consider themselves as having become the Great Sanhedrin of old.

The Sanhedrin and the Jubilee

The Shemitah (the Sabbath rest year) and the Yovel (the Jubilee) are commandments that require Jews to work together. And while the Shemitah was tracked continuously during the exile, the Jubilee was not, and so it would require large-scale coordination to be re-established. The Jubilee, therefore, is a perfect kind of project for the Sanhedrin to study.

They have.

We first learned of the details of this study from one of the Sanhedrin rabbis, Rabbi Avraham Dov ben Shor, who lives in a community in Judea, not far from where Gidon lives. It so happens that Rabbi ben Shor was a member of the working group of the Sanhedrin that studied the Jubilee. I, Bob, found him nothing like the Sanhedrin rabbis of the movies. He was so friendly and warm, so smiling and unassuming, that it took most of the interview before it began to dawn on me that the man in front of me might actually be the leader of the Jubilee project. To this day, I still don't know the answer to that.

Rabbi ben Shor granted us an interview a few weeks ago, and we are excited to now share with you what we learned.

Rabbi Avraham Dov ben Shor (Photo: Root Source)

We asked Rabbi ben Shor why the Sanhedrin took on this Jubilee project.

"Because there is a mitzvah, a commandment, to establish the Shemitah and the Jubilee year."

So we got right down to business and asked him what year does the Sanhedrin think is the Jubilee year?

"We had a large scholarly debate for many months about when it might have been, when it was, and if it's possible. One of the requirements that is often mentioned is that there needs to be a majority of Bnei Yisrael (Jews) living in the land of Israel."

Currently, while Israel has more Jews than any other country, the population has not increased quite to the level where a majority of the world's Jews live in Israel. He went on to say that they see Ezra the Scribe as having re-established the Jubilee year. Why?

"Because the counting of the Shemitah year cannot be established without first establishing the Jubilee year. At some level, Ezra established the counting of the Sabbatical year and the Jubilee year, which go together. There is no fundamental obligation, from the standpoint of the Torah, to let the land lie fallow on the seventh year, if you are not also counting the Jubilee year. [The Sages (the *Anshei Knesset HaGedolah*) do require Shemitah observance as a rabbinical imperative, and it is observed in Israel today as such.] They go together."

When discussing the practical realities of what it might take to re-establish a Jubilee, the rabbi added:

"You have to deal with what exists. That is an important part of a court. You can't just deal with the law, you have to deal with the reality and the situation as it stands, and try to arrive at the *goal* that God sets for you."

In that context, Rabbi ben Shor sees the Jubilee year as very important.

"Do we count from the first year of creation? Do we count from the time of Joshua after he conquered the land? Did it stop during the exile? Did it continue? There are a lot of various opinions of Jewish scholars throughout the ages on all of these."

After discussing all these things over months, they reached their opinion. But before telling us that opinion he quickly added,

"A bigger, better court can always overrule our opinion."

So what was that opinion? The Rabbi continued:

"One of the leading ideas was that this year [5776] should be the Jubilee year. The reason that [year] would fit is that it fits with at least one version of how it's been counted since the time of Ezra. The other reason is because if you count from the time that Jerusalem was redeemed, from the Six-Day War, which would be a logical time to start counting, *this would be the fiftieth year.*"

And yet as soon as he offered us a solution to the Mystery of the Lost Jubilee, he immediately snatched that solution right back from us saying,

"However, we decided that we cannot consider this a Jubilee year."

Why not, we asked? He answered that if they were to consider this a Jubilee year, *they would be violating a commandment of Scripture regarding the Jubilee!*

Can you guess what the problem was in the mind of the Sanhedrin? Looking back and reading Leviticus 25, it is sitting right there as plain as day!

Questions for discussion and thought

Rather than giving the answer away here, we are going to give you the chance to discover and solve this riddle for yourself!

If this is, in fact, a Jubilee year, what commandment would they be violating if they consider this year to be a Jubilee year?

Jimmy Headstream

For this year to be biblically considered a Yovel it would have to have been proclaimed and consecrated on the Day Of Atonement?

Sientje Seinen

My KJV Bible says Leviticus 25 verse 9 "Then thou shalt cause the trumped of the Jubi-lee to sound on the tenth day of the seventh month, in the day of atonement shalt ye make the trumpet sound through all your land." Is it because they did not sound the trumpet throughout the land, the day of atonement was not celebrated?

Sylvia Nichols

I'm guessing that it's because nobody knows who the land should go back to?

Sharon Kerr

23 And the land shall not be sold in perpetuity; for the land is Mine; for ye are strangers and settlers with Me.

Being that the Orthodox Christian Church owns land e.g. Knesset is built on and they have to pay taxes to the Orthodox church. How much land do they own?

The Orthodox Church has extensive property holdings in Jerusalem and throughout Israel and the Palestinian territories. In addition to numerous churches, seminaries and other properties used for religious purposes, church property holdings include the land on which the Knesset and the prime minister's residence are located, as well as an array of historic buildings in Jerusalem's Old City, including the Imperial and Petra hotels inside the Jaffa Gate of the Old City.

Cornell Rhone-Rankin

According to Leviticus 25, the land is supposed to rest in the shemitah and the jubilee. Planting began right after the shemitah ended, which would be a violation.

Ruth Macdonald

I agree with you.

CHAPTER 12

Count Your Blessings

During our interview with Rabbi Avraham Dov ben Shor from the Sanhedrin, we asked him whether, in the opinion of the Sanhedrin, we are currently in a Jubilee year. He told us:

"One of the leading ideas was that this year [5776] should be the Jubilee year. The reason that [this year] would fit is that it fits with at least one version of how it's been counted since the time of Ezra the scribe. The other reason is because if you count from the time that Jerusalem was redeemed, from the Six-Day War, which would be a logical time to start counting, **this would be the fiftieth year**."

And yet as soon as he offered us a solution to the Mystery of the Lost Jubilee, he immediately added the word "however" and said something we had not thought of ourselves. He continued:

"However, we decided that **we cannot start counting retroactively**; that there is no legal precedent to start counting retroactively, even though we could have and perhaps even should have started counting at that year."

In other words, he agreed that they *should have* started counting towards the Jubilee in 1967, but because they did not, they cannot declare this year to be a Jubilee year. The passage in Leviticus 25 clearly requires them to **count** the years.

So the decision of the Sanhedrin?

"We decided that this was not the Jubilee year, but rather that **this is the first year of the counting of the 50**."

And to formally start the counting, they decided to speak a blessing upon this year in Jerusalem. We asked if the blessing was given on Rosh Hashana, the very first day of the year or on Yom Kippur, the tenth day of the year, when the shofar, the ram's horn, was to be blown? He said that the blessing was given in between those two days to allow members of the Sanhedrin around Israel to be able to travel to Jerusalem to participate. (Rosh Hashana and Yom Kippur are treated as a Sabbath rest and so travel is restricted.)

Regarding the blessing, Rabbi ben Shor then smiled broadly and added:

> "I was the one to whom they gave the merit of saying the blessing!"

He said the blessing was neither long nor complicated, but it was written by one of the Sanhedrin members, and included a prayer before and afterwards. The blessing itself was something along the lines of:

"Blessed are you, Lord our God, who commands us in the counting of the Sabbaticals and the Yovels."

We asked how often this counting will happen?

He answered, "Every year. We declare that this is the first year of the counting towards the first Sabbatical year towards the Yovel."

He explained that they decided to follow the pattern of the Counting of the Omer, which counts the 50 days from Passover to Shavuot (which Christians refer to as Pentecost). In that counting, the Jews do not simply count numbers from 1 to 50, but count the days within the weeks as well. So the first day is day one of week one, through day seven of week seven, and finally Shavuot is declared.

But he went on to say that the reason not to declare this year as a Jubilee was more than just technical, it was also practical.

"Practical purposes are also part of the decisions of a court. The Sanhedrin is not accepted by all the nation of Israel. If all of the nation is not on the same page, it doesn't matter. We hope that in 50 years, the idea of a Jewish Sanhedrin will be accepted universally. In 50 years it will either get traction, or it won't. Either way, we will know where we are headed, or not headed."

He then added a twist about the current year.

"By declaring that this is the first year of the counting, we are also saying that this *was* a Jubilee year of the *exile*. Why? Because when you are in exile, you don't count an extra year for the fiftieth year."

So we then asked what happens in 50 years. Will that Jubilee year overlap with the first year of the next cycle, or will that year stand on its own?

"We are discussing that right now in various committees. One of the aspects we are also studying is what does a Jubilee year actually mean in modern life today? Because one of the main aspects of a Jubilee year involve the returning of the family inheritance, the redemption of slavery. All this will be discussed during the next 50 years!"

He then went on to tell us about one major impact an agreement on the Jubilee year has. If it is decided that a Jubilee year is upcoming, then that raises the level of required observance for the Sabbath (or Shemitah) years. They must be followed strictly according to the Torah and not just according to decisions the rabbis made during the exile period.

He concluded by saying,

"God has his own plan. And things tend to fall into place."

Then he smiled and added, "God makes things work even when we don't want Him to! He takes our enemy's thoughts and turns them on their heads to make it work according to His plan. He does that all the time. That does not mean we do not have an obligation to give it our best effort; but we should know that our best effort is *just that*. It is an obligation on our part, not an obligation on God's part to follow our best effort. *He will fit* our best effort into His plan."

The full interview with Rabbi Avraham ben Shor is recorded and available on our website, www.root-source.com/blog/sanhedrin-makes-decision-jubilee-year.

From all of this we can conclude that the Jewish people have many years to decide whether they will celebrate the Jubilee 50 years from now. For the nation of Israel to decide to celebrate it 50 years from now seems like a very big step. This thought, and the rabbi's comment that God often provides help, seems to put a great deal of focus on the current Jewish year we are in, that being 5776 which ends on October 2, 2016.

Perhaps an amazing event regarding Israel before October 2nd would help convince the Jewish people that it is time to come together and figure out how the Jubilee can be brought to life in modern-day Israel. The good news for us, is that we will know one way or another in months, not years! October is just a stone's throw away now.

Fasten your seatbelt and let's see where this ride ends up!

Questions for discussion and thought

What do you think about this interview?

How do you feel about the Sanhedrin's decision to not consider the current Jewish year to be a Jubilee, but rather to be Year One of the counting to a Jubilee in the future?

If the Messiah tarries, do you think all of Israel will celebrate the Jubilee 50 years from now?

Earl W. Littlefield Jr

As a Christian American past my 70th birthday, I do not expect to be here in this present body for 50 more years and I suspect there are many Jewish people in similar situation. Do God's commands for the Jubilee apply to individuals regardless of there being no "Sanhedrin" to count for them? Did the Torah not apply during the dispersal ??? With the return to Israel and the re-instution of the "Sanhedrin", does their ignoring of the requirements of Jubilee while they count absolve them and all Jews of God's commands ???

Joe Wilkerson

Guys, I just don't know what to say here. Like Earl, I'm in my mid seventies now and looking for the rapture and who knows, except God, when that will be. Am I wrong Mr. O'Dell to wonder what's going on now. I really expected that by 50 years from now we would be in the millennial reign of Christ. I hope we get more opinions on this. According to all that I've read and watched the rapture was just around the corner. Like Earl, I will not be here in 50 years. Everyone that I've read says to watch what's going on in Israel and that will show us the way. Help!

Corlia Dupisanie

Dear Earl and Joe, I am 73, and a woman. I don't believe in the rapture, but, being a Christian, I am also waiting for the Christ's Second Coming. I may not live to see it, but I firmly believe that our children (my husband died in 2000) will experience the Second Coming. The Biblical prophecies are being fulfilled one by one.

Daystar Burton

If the Sanhendrin are starting to count this year as the first year, then the Jubilee was last year, it seems that the Sanhedrin are a bit vague about the whole matter. According to Lev. 25:2 'When you come into the land which I give you, then the land shall keep a sabbath to the Lord.' So when do we count from, when the Jewish folks came into the land to posess it when they left Egypt or from the time we returned to the land as a State, May 1948 seems like a good point to start from or possibly 1947 but we must count according to the Hebrew calendar, not the Gregorian one. All our Godly days start in the evening. It seems to me that the God of Israel is an agricultural God counting by the lunar calendar.

Cornell Rhone-Rankin

It seems that the Sanhedrin for whatever reason made the decision not to accept this year as Jubilee. What about GOD? I do not believe that HE did not stop the count, the next Jubilee will be when the Messiah son of David is ruling in Jerusalem. The events of this year will tell the story as stated above. Based on the worldwide financial cycles that have been taking place during the past several shemitahs, wheather man counts, the LORD does.

CHAPTER 13

Blood Moons and Jubilee

In our interview with Rabbi Avraham Dov ben Shor of the Sanhedrin, he told us that the Sanhedrin considers this Hebrew year, 5776, as "Year One" counting toward the next Jubilee. He also said that the counting towards Year One should have theoretically begun in 1967, which would have made *this year* a Jubilee year.

Many people are watching our current year to see if God might reaffirm this year as a Jubilee year through some amazing events. We will continue to monitor current events even after this book is published.

One question that has been raised in the comments to these chapters is whether the recent Blood Moon lunar eclipses that occurred on the nights of Passover and Sukkot in 2014 and 2015 have any connection to the Jubilee. That is the topic of this chapter.

We would propose to you that the answer to that question is both NO and YES!

First, in what sense is there no connection? From a biblical standpoint, the Jubilee cycle and the Shemitah cycle are well defined in Scripture and are only connected to the sun and the moon the sense that the entire Hebrew calendar is connected to the sun and the moon. There is no command related to the Shemitah or the Jubilee that can in any way be modified or altered by the presence of a lunar eclipse occurring on the night of Passover or Sukkot.

But is there any connection? What if we simplify the question and ask, **Has a Blood Moon ever occurred during a Jubilee year?** Here, the answer is a resounding yes!

The Blood Moons that have occurred in the last 2,000 years were in the following years:

162/163 AD

795/796 AD

842/843 AD

860/861 AD

1428/29 AD Jubilee

1493/94 AD

1949/50 AD

1967/68 AD Jubilee

2014/15 AD Jubilee

Looking at all nine of these Blood Moons events, we see an overlap between the Blood Moons and the Jubilee year on three of the nine occasions. The following charts shows how this happened.

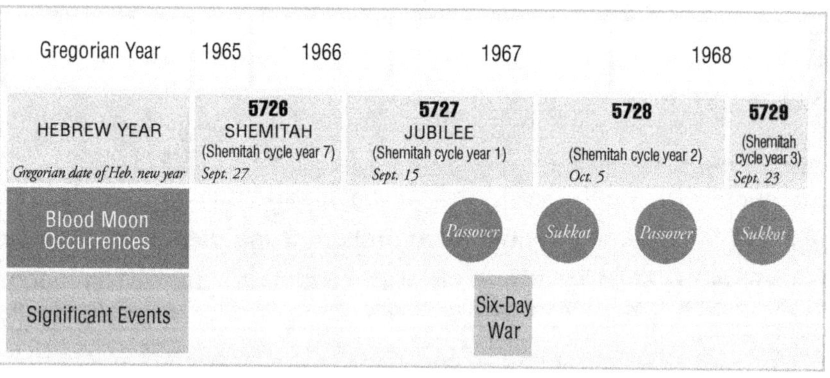

Blood Moons and Jubilee Overlap in 1968 (Chart by Gidon Ariel)

Here we can see in 1967, the Six-Day War and the reunification of Jerusalem occurred during Jewish year 5727, a Jubilee year. The first of the four Blood Moons occurred in that same Jubilee year!

	2013	2014	2015	2016
Gregorian Year				
SHEMITAH / JUBILEE CYCLE YEAR *Gregorian date of Heb. new year*	**5774** (Shemitah cycle year 6) *Sept. 5*	**5775** SHEMITAH (Shemitah cycle year 7) *Sept. 25*	**5776** JUBILEE(?) (Shemitah cycle year 1) *Sept. 14*	**5777** (Shemitah cycle year 2) *Oct. 3*
Blood Moon Occurrences	*Passover*	*Sukkot*	*Passover*	*Sukkot*
Significant Events				?

Blood Moons and Jubilee Overlap in 2015 (Chart by Gidon Ariel)

Then, in 2015, in the early morning hours of Sukkot on September 28, the final Blood Moon occurred in what we have proposed here might well be another Jubilee year!

Besides the fact that they occurred at the same time, is there actually a *spiritual* connection between the meaning of the Blood Moons and Jubilee? The answer to that depends on the meaning of the Blood Moons themselves, because the meaning of the Jubilee from Scripture is clear: it is about *return* and *release*.

What is the meaning of the Blood Moons? The most commonly held view of the Blood Moons, championed by authors John Hagee and Mark Biltz, is that they:

- Come before a great and terrible Day of the Lord

- Signal judgment to the enemies of Israel

- Signal war with Israel

If you accept that, then you could say that the spiritual connection between the Blood Moons and Israel is this: *if an amazing event happens* *in Israel before October 3rd, and that amazing event **involves a war against Israel,*** then everything lines up.

Before now we have not discussed our opinion of the Blood Moons in this book. But after carefully studying the Scriptures, history, and science, and not just the past few Blood Moons but *all* of them in the last 2,000 years, we have revealed an exciting pattern of God's provision for the Jews in the times of the Blood Moons in our book, *Israel FIRST!* Each wave of Blood Moons that occurs in history signals an exodus of Jews from one part of the world to another. Our discovery was that, much like the pattern of the original Exodus, the most critical times for the Jews occur *before* Blood Moons, not after. This is exactly what happened in 1492, in 1948, and in 1967. Not all Blood Moons resulted in war, and historically, none of the sets of four Blood Moons preceded a major war. Rather, the Blood Moons would be better seen as times of celebration and relief!

Based on our understanding of the meaning of the Blood Moons, we might say that: *whatever amazing events that might happen in Israel relating to the Jubilee, will **not** come about as the result of a major war against Israel, at least not a war of similar magnitude to the Six-Day War.*

Now, of course, our opinion could be wrong. We want Israel to have the benefit of the Jubilee, and to have property restored, but we are essentially asking, praying, *pleading* with God to do this amazing work without the need for an immediate war against the nation of Israel!

You may have already decided in your own mind that the Gog and Magog war will begin in the next year or two, and that Israel will gain the territory it has been promised by God through that war. You could be right! But, would it not be even more amazing if God were to accomplish something huge for Israel *without* a major conflict in 2016 or 2017? That goes beyond our opinion, it is our prayer, even as we must all be praying for the peace of Jerusalem.

Last, we will end this chapter with a tone of inspiration rather than a tone of war. But the inspiration actually comes from a story that involves war.

We have discussed General Allenby and his march into Jerusalem during World War I on December 11, 1917. We have also said that this event, along with the Balfour Declaration a few weeks earlier, both occurred in what seems to have been a year of Jubilee. And what does this have to do with the Blood Moons, you might ask?

The answer is: nothing.

Or so we thought.

But during the last Blood Moon on the early morning hours of September 28, 2015, the only Blood Moon of the four that was visible in Israel, we tried to photograph that Blood Moon from inside Jerusalem, and even more than that, we decided to try to recreate the General Allenby photograph from 1917.

And the result?

September 28, 2015, Blood Moon from Jerusalem and General Allenby Enters Jerusalem (Photos: Root Source and Wikicommons)

So while we did expect to capture the Blood Moon over the Jaffa Gate, imagine our surprise when we realized that the position of the moon was in the very same position as the old Ottoman clock tower that was torn down by the British in 1922!

Is God trying to *wake us up* to the Jubilee and events like the Blood Moons and his plans for Israel and the World?

May those who have eyes to see, be given the chance to enjoy the move of God on this earth. And like we said last time, fasten your seatbelt and let's see where this ride takes us!

Questions for discussion and thought

What does this photograph say to you?

Are there any other ways in which the Blood Moons and Jubilee year might be related, that we might have missed?

Marilyn Kline

Fantastic pictures. God is very subtle sometimes. The blood moon is right in the same place as the clock was. Looking backwards in time we can see the hand of God, but trying to predict Him in the future, that's much much harder.

Samantha Mandy Elkins

Erm.

1. The blood moon looks like a JAFFA orange.

2. This installs the moon cycle as more important today than the time piece!!

3. But the British live by the time piece?

Laurence Bosma

http://bloodmoonscoming.com/?page_id=593

Dennis McLeod

Hertzl declaration 1897 50 years to 1947. 1917 Balfour declaration to 1967 Israel gets back Jerusalem. Counting from 67 in my maths makes it 49 and 1 + 2017, then what?

CHAPTER 14

Jubilee on a Mission

In the last chapter, we showed how the Jubilee may have overlapped the last two Blood Moons cycles. We will now look at a topic that you might never have predicted would appear in this book: Christian missions.

If there is a Jubilee cycle that is present in the years of 1917 and 1967, and if in fact we are currently in a Jubilee year in 2016, then we ought to be able to see more examples of key events happening in the wake of those years in other areas of the world besides just Israel. We look at Israel and the Jews first for clues as to the Jubilee years, but should not part of God's pattern include restoration and release in the Christian world as well?

This brings us to the topic of missions.

One of our readers, Allan Johnson has offered us the following insights. He says some key events in Christian missions tied back to some of the earliest Jubilee years we mentioned.

First, he checked into the life of **William Carey** and his work in India. Carey has often been called the father of modern Christian missions. He did not find any significant events in his life that fit the pattern of the Jubilee years.

Next he checked the life of **Hudson Taylor**, well-known for his work in China.

James Hudson Taylor
(Photo: Wikipedia)

Allan writes to us:

At first I found nothing all that obvious for Hudson Taylor. It wasn't the starting point of his work in China, or the date of any of his journeys back to China from England. But there was a book called *Hudson Taylor's Spiritual Secret* containing a chapter called "The Exchanged Life" which describes what seems to have been a pivotal point in his life. At that point, through a letter from a colleague, God illuminated Hudson Taylor's understanding of how to truly walk with Him in faith — simply resting in Him and depending on His strength. This is very much like what a Jubilee year is meant for — a time for fully resting in God's provision. So when was that turning point for him? Sept 4, 1869, which is within the final month of one of the proposed Jubilee years. This new perspective stayed with him for the rest of his life, empowering him in leading the work in China for over 30 more years.

And that is not all. Allan also told us about **Cam Townsend**, often considered the father of modern-day Bible translation.

Allan writes:

In 2013 I had researched the origin of SIL International, which studies foreign languages for the purpose of Bible translation.

After this Jubilee article series, I went back through my notes, and the date 1917/18 caught my attention. It turns out that this Jubilee time period was a significant time of processing for Cam Townsend, bringing

William Cameron Townsend
(Photo: Wikipedia)

him to a conclusion and vision that he recorded in his diary on Aug 30, 1918, once again at the end of a Jubilee year. As a result he travelled to a people group of Guatemala, translated the Bible for them, and then with this experience behind him, was led to found an organization to work toward doing this very same thing for people groups all over the world who didn't yet have access to the Bible.

As if this were not interesting enough, Allan's ideas then spurred Bob to check *his* notes regarding the first successful mission movement to a Muslim people group. His research from 2013 revealed that a native Indonesian Muslim named Radin Abas Sadrach Surapranata, later famously called "Sadrach, the Apostle of Java," had a turning point in his life when he received his "divine call" to preach the gospel to the local Muslim inhabitants.

Sadrach: The Apostle of Java.
(Photo: archive.org)

Sadrach later said that this divine call was as pivotal in his life as the biblical call of Abraham was to Abraham. Sadrach would become the first man in the history of the world to guide more than 1,000 Muslims to exchange Islam for Christianity. He would also become an early model for indigenous missions (guided by locals, rather than by sending organizations). And the date of that divine call? In the late 1868 to early 1869 timeframe, putting it once again in a Jubilee year!

Certainly we are not claiming that the important things only happen in Jubilee years. But a pattern of cases found so quickly for significant missions leaders is notable.

Now with this talk of missions in a book co-written by a Jew and a Christian, you are probably wondering how Gidon, as an Orthodox Jew reacts to this topic? Clearly, ideas for our articles must be agreed upon by Gidon! Here is Gidon on why he is willing to have this material covered in our series:

"Jews tend to think in a self-focused manner when it comes to missionary activity. Jews, when they hear the word missionary, they think "Christians trying to get Jews to be Christians." However, most Christian missionary activity throughout history has naturally been aimed at non-Jews, by mere availability and geography. For example, here is an extensive website about missions that barely mentions the word Jews or Israel: http://www.aboutmissions.org/statistics.html.

If missionary activity can be seen and characterized as introducing people to the God of Abraham (albeit with a strong dose of non-Jewish Christian theology) — the mandate of the Jewish people since the Sinaitic Covenant — then Jews should be grateful to Christians who have picked up their (understandable) slack for the past two millennia while the Jews were busy surviving (tragically, often from persecution from those same Christians or their coreligionists).

The thunderous changes in the world over the past few hundreds of years, and especially over the past few dozens of years, would point to Jews rethinking their position regarding Christians missionizing to others, especially those Christian missionaries who are more knowledgeable and sensitive about the place of Jews, Israel and Jewish wisdom in God's plan.

This, then, is exactly the mandate of the organization we founded — Root Source — to empower Christians with the Jewish wisdom and relationships with Jews that have been missing pretty much since Christianity's founding."

Questions for discussion and thought

Have you found any interesting tie-ins between the dates discussed in this article series and your own research?

Thanks to Allan Johnson for providing the research on Hudson Taylor and Cam Townsend mentioned in this chapter. Allan can be reached through his blog at https://snofriacus.wordpress.com/.

Maria Yvonne Tan

Definitely, 1917 and 1830 are significant years in Catholic History, the first one, because of Fatima and the miracle of the Sun and the second was the Miraculous Medal that saved many lives during WW I.

DrDiane M Hoffmann

Great article... speaking of current events and this 2016 year... I think a major thing happening right now is this awful planting of the Baal arches in London and in New York. It seems interesting that the one in London is being set-up in the Spring of this year and the other will be New York in the Fall. I think that we will be seeing a fast downhill after this, notwithstanding this following the satanic statue that was erected in Detroit just a few months ago. That's pretty serious.

Carolyn Southam

I was born again on 8 June 1968. Definitely a key event, or, THE key event in my life. Went to church and Sunday school for years, read a King James with tiny print from Genesis to Revelation as soon as I could read (loved the stories about the patriarchs), but one weekend someone travelled to our state to preach the gospel and a couple of older ladies took a group of young people to hear him. From the back of the crowded hall, I felt for the first time that Jesus was asking me to respond to Him. At first I wondered why the entire audience there didn't go forward publically, because the call was so strong, but thought afterwards that perhaps they were already saved. So it was just within a year of the six-day war. Have often wondered whether the blessing in Israel was followed by a spiritual blessing to the Gentiles.

CHAPTER 15

Readers Respond

After showing how the proposed Jubilee years of 1917/18 and 1868/69 overlapped with some turning points in Christian missions activity, we asked for any other interesting examples noticed by readers.

Reader Hal Brooks then wrote us the following:

I have enjoyed your series of articles on Jubilee. It is important news that the Sanhedrin has started the Yovel count from this year! I agree that 1966/67 was a Jubilee "event" for Israel with the restoration of Judea, Samaria, and most importantly Jerusalem to full Israeli control. Before that 1917/18 brought the Balfour Declaration and British defeat of the Ottoman Empire.

I would like to point out the following strong support that 1868/69 also involved a Jubilee "event" that you have not yet discussed. In Deuteronomy 29:22 there is a reference to a "foreigner" who will come from afar, confirm the desolation of the Land, and proclaim it to the nations.

That indeed happened exactly as prophesied when Samuel Clemens (Mark Twain) published his best selling work The Innocents Abroad in…. 1869!

Indeed, Mark Twain has become a commonly quoted source for Zionists

Mark Twain
(Photo: AF Bradley, Wikicommons)

and Jewish educators. The series of articles he wrote for a San Francisco newspaper were published as a subscription book on July 20, 1869, within that Jubilee year. That book, *The Innocents Abroad*, also called *The New Pilgrim's Progress*, which included an eye witness description of his travels to the Holy Land, became one of the best-selling travel books of all time.

Hal continues by quoting book passages from *Innocents Abroad* he finds remarkable:

There is not a solitary village throughout its whole extent — not for 30 miles in either direction. There are two or three small clusters of Bedouin tents, but not a single permanent habitation. One may ride ten miles hereabouts and not see ten human beings. To this region one of the prophecies is applied: "I will bring the Land into desolation; and your enemies which dwell therein shall be astonished at it. And I will scatter you among the heathen, and I will draw out a sword after you; and your Land shall be desolate and your cities waste." No man can stand here by deserted Ain Mellahah and say the prophecy has not been fulfilled. (page 349)

There is one thing he (the Wandering Jew) cannot avoid; go where he will about the world, he must never fail to report in Jerusalem every fiftieth year. (page 418)

Hal then comments, "I find these passages to be remarkable fulfillments of Bible prophecy. They directly affect the Land and the restoration of Israel! It is marvelous to witness these events within a Jubilee context."

Thank you, Hal for that insight into the timing, as well as the suggestion that Mark Twain's trip was not only a verification of biblical prophecy, but a fulfilling of biblical prophecy!

This important book from Mark Twain fits within the repeating pattern of the Jubilee, coming on the fiftieth year of the counting, yet repeating every 49 years.

Fifty and One Hundred Year Patterns

However, we are aware that many of our readers are of the persuasion to only look for Jubilee patterns 50 and 100 years apart. For those who enjoy seeing interesting correlations to the Gregorian calendar, 50 and 100 years apart, we note that while Mark Twain's work was **published** in 1869, his actual **visit** to the Holy Land was in 1867. This was 50 years before the Balfour Declaration and 100 years before the reunification of Jerusalem in 1967.

Speaking of 50-year cycles, reader Dennis McLeod reminded us that we have not mentioned the famous diary entry by Jewish Zionist leader Theodor Herzl, who wrote on September 1, 1897, just one day following the conclusion of the First Zionist Congress in Basel, Switzerland:

> At Basel I founded the Jewish State. If I said this out loud today I would be greeted by universal laughter. In five years perhaps, and certainly in **fifty** years, everyone will recognize it.

Herzl was correct. United Nations resolution 181, passed 50 years later on November 29, 1947, created legal grounds for the formation of a Jewish State, putting an end to the laughter. The Sanhedrin Rabbi we talked to told us that they considered the reunification of Jerusalem more important from a Jubilee-counting perspective than the establishment of the State of Israel in 1948. However, the establishment is clearly an event of momentous proportions in its own right.

The fact that the reunification of Jerusalem and the re-establishment of the state of Israel, could not possibly be considered to *both* be on the same Jubilee cycle (because they are only 19 years apart) shows that

God is not limited to do His work on only Jubilee years.

This is an important point.

Jubilee and Messiah

No reader of this book will ever catch us making a suggestion that the Jubilee years under discussion forecast the coming of the Messiah. We know that God can and will do whatever He wants, and that ultimately God's timing will be perfect in its own right, even if His actions have nothing whatever to do with the timing of earth's Jubilee years.

Israel Knesset building
(Photo: Sherwood Burton)

For readers to hope that the Messiah's coming will be in an imminent Jubilee year is a good thing, because hoping for the Messiah is *always* a good thing. It is also *just* as important not to lose hope if we complete a Jubilee year and nothing significant happens regarding the Messiah's arrival. Our hope and expectation honors God much more, we would suggest, than the predictions of any certain year in which His coming might happen. Our hope and expectation should not be diminished by the year in which we are living. It should only increase more and more over time.

It is good and right for this book to attempt to discover the true nature of the Jubilee, because God invented it, and because it is the glory of kings to search out a matter which God has hidden (see Proverbs 25:2). Any additional connection to the Messiah is terribly exciting for sure, but that is a deeper mystery than might ever be revealed on this earth, let alone in this book. So in the meantime, let us simply work to solve the mystery right before us, a mystery that seems to be very close to being revealed by the hand of God. So let us simply see what we might find.

Joani Hoover

One hundred years before the 1967 war in Israel when the world watched amazed as Israel regained their capital of Jerusalem, the slaves were set free in the USA at around that time after the Civil War was over. That is one of the statutes of the Jubilee year to let the slaves go free. I think it is awesome that God's calendar continues even though many of the Christian faith don't believe those things are applicable anymore. THEY ARE!

Betty Williamson

Count me in

Thank you for this scholarly exchange of ideas... together as One New Man as per Proverbs 25:2. What a lovely adventure!

Dennis Wright

Count me in, it is great to see so many examples of prophecy being fulfilled we can have no doubt that the final redemption is just around the corner.

Lynda M Sipes

I have not had the advantage of previously studying anything in depth about the jubilee year so my knowledge is very limited. I am really appreciating the enlightenment of your articles in this series!!!

Allan Johnson

Wow - that connection to Mark Twain is pretty cool. I wonder if he realised that he was fulfilling Scripture.

Also "liked" and made comments:

Pat Hogan
Laurence Bosma
Johnny Ash
Leo de Silva
Fred Rymer III

Jubilees Across Time

Do today's Jubilee years connect back to when the Israelites entered the Land of Canaan under Joshua?

And the definitive answer to that question is: "pause, sound of clearing of throat, ahem, uhm, well…."

Because the answer is that there is no definitive answer to this simple question — a question that is so appropriate, so obvious that even a child might ask it. Did God not say, "when you come into the land which I shall give you"? (Leviticus 25:2)

Simple but Difficult

Here are the reasons that this simple question is so profoundly difficult to answer.

First, the identity of the year that Joshua crossed the Jordan river with the Children of Israel to enter the land is not universally agreed upon. For the moment, let us explore the Jewish tradition through *Seder Olam*.

Seder Olam is the famous Jewish book which made the first *written* attempt to put together a chronology of time from creation until the day of its writing, around 100 CE. The *Seder Olam*, still followed today, gives us the current Jewish year of 5776 since creation. The Jewish tradition of *Seder Olam* has Joshua's entry at year 2488.

Jordan River at the site of Joshua's crossing (Photo: Bob O'Dell)

Second, the Children of Israel did not settle down immediately, but had to conquer the land in a series of battles. That took time. Jewish tradition is that they spent the first seven years conquering the Land and the next seven years dividing the land between tribes and appropriating the land to the various families within the tribes. That would mean that "Year One" of the counting would not have occurred until 14 years after entry.

If that is the case, then Year One would be in 2488 + 14 = 2502.

So let's continue within the Jewish chronology and see how that year fits. The number of years that have passed since that Year One is 5776 (this year) - 2502 (Year One) = 3274 years. If you start counting from that Year One in multiples of 49, the last Jubilee was 40 years ago in 1976, which does not fit any of the key dates in Jewish history that have been discussed in this book. And you have another, bigger problem, which is that the Shemitah cycles don't fit either. None of the Jewish Shemitah cycles being counted for more than 2,000 years match — they are all off by two years.

Can we solve the problem if we count by 50 years rather than 49? No.

What about the Jewish exile, and the idea that the land had to rest for 70 years? If we were to stop counting Shemitah years during the 70 years of exile, does it solve the problem of the Jubilee dates? No, that puts the last Jubilee in 2004.

More Difficulties Explained

Now for another twist. The *Seder Olam* and archeological records are in disagreement over the date of the destruction of Solomon's Temple. Archeology dates that event to 586 BCE, give or take a year. However, the *Seder Olam* dates it to the year 3338 which equals about 422 BC, a difference of 164 years. Let us suppose that Seder Olam is wrong on this point, but correct on everything else. If we were to factor in this gap of 164 years, does that solve our problem? No, it puts the Jubilee in 2008, which also does not match key events in Jewish history. One of our readers, chronology researcher Jim Lewis, suggests *Jewish History in Conflict: A Study of the Major Discrepancy between Rabbinic and Conventional Chronology*, by Mitchell First, for further study on that 164-year gap.

Another Jewish tradition that is not aligned perfectly with *Seder Olam* is that Adam was created in Year One, rather than before the start of the calendar. That would add 1 to all the dates. Another Jewish opinion is that Year One was a short year — only the seven days of creation — so it would cause the addition of two years to *Seder Olam* dates.

And there are many more variations that have been proposed that generally fall into one of three categories:

(1) Finding other "mistakes" in *Seder Olam*, (in addition to the 164-year gap) that when added together cause important dates of history to fit on nice Jubilee boundaries — the coming into the land, all the way up to the presently celebrated Shemitah years and modern "assumed Jubilee" years such as 1967.

(2) Using *Seder Olam*, but positing that the existing Jewish Shemitah years got off-cycle somehow, and concluding that the Shemitah cycle being followed in Israel today must be fixed. We find this solution very unappealing for a few reasons:

    a. There is strong evidence that the Shemitah cycles have been kept since the time of Ezra. Why should we assume that their decisions would be unaligned with the past? At least the Shemitah cycles would have been known, if not the Jubilee.

    b. Getting the nation of Israel to change its Shemitah cycle would be nearly impossible after over 2,000 years of keeping it in a certain way.

    c. There is natural evidence that the existing Shemitah cycles *are* correct, and that the pattern of Jubilee-type events occurring in 1967 and 1917 fits perfectly with those same Shemitah cycles that have been kept for thousands of years. If the existing Shemitah cycles were so off-base, then why would God seem to be corroborating them with divine providence in 1917 and 1967?

(3) Concluding that the work of God today is a new work, and therefore we should not even attempt to connect to the past. This opinion results in a discussion about the character of God

Himself. Our view is that the work of God on the earth is perfect and majestic. He has shown time and time again how He works through history and ties events together in a perfect way that is nothing less than the work of a master artist. Why should Jubilees across time be exempt from His artistry?

Our Opinion

It would make us feel much better if the Jubilee dates tied back to dates of the past. The current Shemitah cycle of the Jewish calendar *does* seem to be consistent since the time of Nehemiah and Ezra, who called for the people of Israel to hear the law after the exile, to remember the covenant, and to dedicate themselves to keeping the Sabbath years. While there is no mention of the Jubilee in those books, the pattern of the Shemitah was reestablished, and one view proposed by today's Jewish Sanhedrin was that the Jubilees were *counted* in the time of Ezra, even if they were not *celebrated*. In addition, some researchers find evidence that the Sabbath years identified by Josephus in his writings in the first century do fit perfectly with the Shemitah years of today, making it reasonable to assume that they also tie back a few hundred more years to the time of Nehemiah and Ezra.

It's not just us. There seems to be a common theme that many people want to solve this problem, including our readers and chronologists around the world. In fact, the Jewish writers of the apocryphal Book of Jubilees, written in the second century BC, put forward a whole history and chronology from Adam to Joshua's entering the land. This book counts Jubilees in 49-year cycles (as we have often proposed in this article series), but it actually puts forward a chronology that has the Children of Israel entering the land in year 2450, on exactly the fiftieth Jubilee from creation! While this book is not canonized and has inconsistencies when compared to the Hebrew Bible, our point is about intent! A writer 22 centuries ago wanted to see everything fit together in a harmonious way, just as we are discussing here.

We are not saying everything *must* fit, but rather that there seems to be a *yearning* to make it fit. Is there any reasonable chronology that:

- Is consistent with all of Scripture

- Finds Joshua going into the land on a "Jubilee from creation"

- Once the counting begins (perhaps in the fourteenth year), aligns to the existing Shemitah years and the year 1967 as a Jubilee?

It seems never to have been done. Will it ever be done?

Questions for discussion and thought

Do you understand *now* why the Jubilee has caused so much frustration and confusion among Jewish and Christian chronology researchers over hundreds if not thousands of years?

Dave Roland

A thought provoking article, well done guys! Looking forward to the next in the series.

Johnny Ash

A Jubilee is 50 years (49 + 1); the fiftieth year is also the 1st year of the next cycle. From circa 1415 BCE when Joshua son of Nun entered the land to 2016 CE is 70 Jubilee'. Be ready; as a wise virgin.

Marilyn Kline

The biggest possession the Jews got back was Israel, in May of 1948. I am surprised it doesn't seem to fit in as a Jubilee Year either, but maybe the 1917-18 events are counted as part of the founding of The State of Israel. Fascinating work. Obviously God can't be wrong, so it must be something on the human side of things. Keep it up! I love reading and contemplating our God and His relationship to Israel, then the ripples come out to the whole world from there.

CHAPTER 17

The Eternal Golan

The Golan Heights, Israel's mountainous northern region, is one of the most beautiful and most traveled parts of the country. It also is a critically strategic area, that commands the entire north of Israel.

Israel captured the Golan Heights from Syria in the Six-Day War in 1967 and in 1981 extended Israeli law to the region, essentially annexing it.

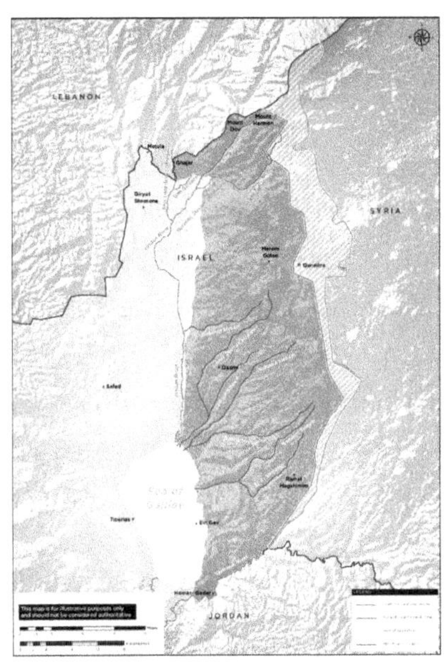

The Golan Heights (map courtesy MFA.gov.il)

That annexation was never recognized by the world, and even Israel has at times considered the Golan a potential bargaining chip it might employ in peace negotiations.

On Sunday April 17, 2016, Prime Minister Benjamin Netanyahu made history by holding the first-ever official cabinet meeting on the other side of the Sea of Galilee, in the Golan Heights. At that meeting he declared to the entire world, "The Golan will forever remain in Israel's hands."

Netanyahu had, in the past, according to multiple Israeli news sources, held secret discussions with Syria about the future of this region both in 1998, and again in 2010, prior to the beginning of the Arab Spring.

However, with the devolution of war-torn Syria and the onset of talks in Geneva about whether a diplomatic solution could be reached in Syria, it was time to change positions and to move quickly.

A statement from Netanyahu's government needed to be made, because the UN does not recognize the Golan as part of Israel, and most if not all parties in the Syrian negotiations would propose adding the Golan into the set of lands that would end up being divvied up among all parties. It would be a prize too valuable to ignore and Netanyahu wanted no part in encouraging it.

"The time has come for the international community to recognize reality," Netanyahu said at the cabinet meeting held in the Jewish village of Ma'ale Gamla. "First, no matter what will be on the other side of the border, the border will not change. Second, the time has come after **50 years** for the international community to finally recognize that the Golan Heights will remain **forever** under Israeli sovereignty." He added, "For the 19 years that the Golan was under Syrian occupation, it served as a place for bunkers, barbed wires, mines and aggression — it was used for war. In the **49 years** that the Golan has been under Israeli control it was used for agriculture, tourism, economic initiatives, and building — it was used for peace." (emphasis added)

Netanyahu gave John Kerry a 12-hour advance notice of his upcoming statement, speaking with him on Saturday night. According to a report by the *Jerusalem Post,* Netanyahu told Kerry that he doubted Syria would ever return to what it was before the civil war that began in that country in 2011.

The United States wasted no time announcing on Monday, April 18, that it does not recognize the Golan as being part of Israel. The UN Security Council then held a meeting on the matter on Tuesday, April 26, and formally stated:

Golan agriculture seen from an Israeli hilltop. Syria can be seen in the distance. (Photo: Bob O'Dell)

"The members recall Resolution 497 [which] decided that the Israeli decision to impose its laws, jurisdiction and administration in the occupied Syrian Golan Heights is null and void and without international and legal effect."

A Golan Jubilee

A number of points can be made with regard to the statements above concerning this potential Jubilee year.

What is *really* at issue here, of course, is the right of Israel to annex more of its historic homeland. Having Golan under Israeli control has only increased Israel's claim to the land. In the years since the liberation of the Golan, dozens of ancient synagogues found there prove a thriving Jewish population existed there in the past. The fact that small amounts of oil have also been discovered in the Golan do not decrease its importance either.

Second, it is interesting that Netanyahu referred to the land as having been under Israeli control for 50 years — 49 to be exact. Was he aware of the principle of the Jubilee and purposely rounded 49 up to 50 years for that very purpose? For most world leaders we wouldn't consider this, but for Netanyahu, a student of history and the son of a history professor, this would seem entirely possible.

Third, we find it fascinating that in order for this meeting to be in the Golan, it had to be held on the other side of the Sea of Galilee, meaning that it was "on the other side of the Jordan." **This was the first official governmental meeting in the modern history of Israel that was ever held on the east side of the Jordan!**

And according to the boundaries of God's original promise to Abraham as well as future promises such as in Ezekiel 47, it won't be the last. Much Israeli ground, to be gained at some point in the future, will be on the east side as well.

Golan Heights as seen from Tiberias on the Sea of Galilee (Photo: Bob O'Dell)

Fourth, unlike all but one other cabinet member who joined him, Netanyahu was driven to the meeting in his own vehicle. This meant he crossed over the Jordan River on a bridge on Sunday, presumably returning later that day. This allowed him to "re-enter the land" reminiscent of the footsteps of Joshua, **who had claimed the ground on the east side of the Jordan first, and only then crossed the Jordan**.

We don't know whether Netanyahu left Ma'ale Gamla immediately after the meeting on Sunday afternoon, but if he waited until sundown on Sunday to cross, he would have crossed the Jordan river on Nissan 10, the same day that Joshua crossed the Jordan river so many years ago! According to Joshua 4:19:

Now the people came up from the Jordan on the tenth of the first month, and camped at Gilgal on the eastern edge of Jericho.

Fifth, on the very next day after the cabinet meeting, Monday, April 18th in the afternoon of Nissan 10, the first-ever official celebration of Joshua's crossing of the Jordan was held on the banks of the Jordan, about 100 kilometers south of the Galilee at Qasr al Yehud. The creation of this celebration was a combined effort between religious, political and military leaders. (See our Root Source blog http://root-source.com/blog/first-ever-celebration-of-joshuas-crossing/ for a detailed description of that event.) It is fascinating that just like the original crossing with its immediate celebration, this celebration at Qasr al Yehud only occurred after a decision was made to take certain lands on the east side of the Jordan. History repeated itself.

Our View

In this year of 2016 we have been looking to see if God would do something amazing.

Now to be fair, this declaration does not have the same "amazement factor" as the declaration in 1967 that Jerusalem was the eternal capital of Israel. Rather than using the adjective "amazing" in this case, we would rather call this clearly "notable."

An event at this level of importance would be the smallest kind of declaration we would expect to see in a Jubilee year. We will definitely be watching and hoping for more!

But, when you think about it, what Israel has just officially said to the world is that.

"Golan is to Israel as Jerusalem is to Israel."

"It is eternally part of our homeland. No nation will ever take this from us, even by force."

Those are powerful statements. Yet having said that, while it is clear that Netanyahu does not want to give up any land on his watch, we equally believe that Netanyahu does not want to extend the borders of Israel under his watch either. Were that to happen, then God must orchestrate a situation that forces Netanyahu to act on behalf of Israel's safety. It is the only way. Netanyahu knows that land comes only with heartache and problems, at least initially. For Netanyahu to take more land, he must be able to face his nation and say to them with absolute resolve, "This was the only way forward."

Therefore, when we look at the implications of a Jubilee year, and what additional ground might be added, we are essentially agreeing that our request is a very tall order for the approximately five calendar months (as of this writing) remaining in this Jewish year. For the purposes of a Jubilee year, that *is* the bad news.

The good news is that if God so desires, five months is plenty of time.

Questions for discussion and thought

Are you excited about Golan being permanently part of Israel, the first permanent Israeli land taken on the east side of the Jordan River?

Do you consider it important that this event preceded the anniversary of Joshua's crossing of the Jordan by a single day?

Will there be, in your opinion, any negative consequences to nations that belong to the UN Security Council, who unanimously rejected the Israeli claim to the Golan? How might God respond to them?

What else should we be watching for on the east side of the Jordan in the coming months and years?

Clive Campbell

Thank you for the idea of a Jubilee year 49 years after 1967. Remember that God's initial calendar began with Nissan. I too think that big things are going to happen in 2016, but for different reasons. You can read about them under my name at www.faithwriters.com. I am expecting that Israel with expand into Syria past Damascus, onto the East Bank (Gilead) and into Lebanon up to the Litani River, I think. They will also wrongly drive the Palestinians into Jordan, which will lead to the 4th temple--after Solomon's, Zerubbabel's and Herod's. 4 is the number for Israel, for its 4 millennia--1970 BC to 2030 AD. Same with 40, for Israel's 40 centuries. Maranatha, Clive Campbell

Just as a follow-up to my first comment, I note that there are exactly 40 49-year periods from 70 AD to 2030 AD. Is that significant? I wouldn't be surprised.

Rebecca Bonnell

So pleased that Benjamin Netanyahu is keeping the Golan Heights under Jewish Occupation and not giving in to Israel's enemies...Whatever reservations anyone has about Benyamin Netanyahu, He IS a Man of GOD and a Great Leader, Bless Him. XXX

Marilyn Kline

The next big event I am expecting this Jubilee Year, and while obama is still 'in power' in my country, is the Gog/Magog War. A little child 'died' and came back from Heaven and told you the same thing. It's coming soon, and it will be a short war, is what he said.

I pray to God Almighty that it isn't the USA who invades Israel! I still say to the 'far north' of Jerusalem is Moscow! The Russians moved troops around but didn't send any back to Russia, as they told Bibi they were going to. I hope if Obama gave an order to attack Israel, that everyone in the military would say no.

Don't make light of all that oil in the Golan, newly discovered. It is said to be HUGE! Russia would surely like some nearby oil for it's new warm water port there in Syria!

If 'it' begins with a huge earthquake, know that God is on the scene, and His weapons are listed at the end of Ezekiel 38. The King James version of most Christians' Bibles says some would be left alive, but other translations say that is NOT in the original text.

I hope no one dies in Israel as a result of this attack, but when God shows up and decimates the enemies for you, every Jew around the world will be clamoring to make Aliyah!!! And there will be such newfound respect for HaShem, perhaps that will lead directly to your Third Temple building permission!

CHAPTER 18

Let the Oppressed Go Free

How would you react to the news that your dream and wish of thirty years has been granted?

This is not just the theme of some Hollywood movie, but finally the redemptive reality for one heroic man and his family; for hundreds of thousands of people who prayed and worked for his freedom; and possibly for the entire world.

Please forgive me for the hyperbole, but as one of those workers and prayers, allow me, Gidon, to add to that dream come true a new topic that is beginning to grab the imagination of Bible believers worldwide, and you might agree with me before the end of this article.

We are talking about the case of Jonathan Pollard, and his release from prison after 30 years.

Jonathan was a civilian employee of the US Navy in the 1980's, who clandestinely provided Israel with intelligence that the US was under agreement to provide but wasn't providing. The details of the case are debated in court of law and the court of public opinion (see www.jonathanpollard.org for Pollard's advocates' perspective; none of his detractors have anywhere near as rich and detailed a web presence). But in Israel, and especially among the religious Zionists whose ranks he joined while still in prison in the early 90's, he is the symbol of someone who has done his time at the very least; a wrongly punished man in the eyes of many; and to some a veritable modern day Joseph in Egypt — a saint whose incarceration is an atonement for all of us.

Countless grateful wellwishers have been praying for Jonathan's health and release for decades. Nonprofit organizations have been set up to support efforts to cut his sentence short and spread knowledge of his predicament (full disclosure: I was an early director of one of the first such organizations). But year after year, these efforts and prayers went unanswered: for decades no American president agreed to set Jonathan free.

Until now.

In a surprise move, the Parole Commission finally allowed Jonathan Pollard to walk out of Butner Prison in North Carolina on November 20, 2015. The terms of his parole forbid him from leaving U.S. soil for his beloved adopted home Israel for the next five years, but his supporters are not giving up hope that this decision too will be speedily reversed.

NOW THIS is a happy ending for Pollard and company, but I hinted at something more cosmic in the introduction to this article. What salvation of biblical proportions could be related to this?

I present you with Jubilee.

As described in Leviticus 25 and mentioned in other places in the Bible, the Jubilee year, occurring once every 49-50 years, is a universal year of freedom. Apart from the laws of liberation of farmland and real estate that are identical to those of the Shemitah sabbatical year, the Jubilee's main element is the required emancipation of all slaves and captives. (An expanded description of the Jubilee is provided in my recent book, *Israel FIRST! The Key to Understanding the Blood Moons, Shemitah, Promises to Israel, and the Coming Jubilee*.)

Interestingly, according to the Bible and post-biblical records, there is no indication that this national commandment has ever been observed. And because of the Jewish People's exile from their Land, it's very calculation has been lost and is a subject of rabbinic academic debate.

But as numerous bestselling authors have pointed out, candidates for recent Jubilee years were 1966-67 and 1917-18 [Jewish/Biblical years span from September to September], years of significance in Jewish/Israeli history. Five decades since then bring us to today. And more and more people are fascinated by the convergence of tumultuous events this year, further firing imaginations that we might be on the verge of the Jubilee.

How fitting it is that the Jewish People's most famous contemporary prisoner is being released at the beginning of this potential Jubilee year? By none other than the United States, whose very symbol accentuates the focus of the commandment in Leviticus: "proclaim liberty throughout all the land unto all the inhabitants thereof"!

This year has not officially been pronounced by Jewish authorities as the year of the Jubilee; many other more pressing issues are still awaiting renewal and decision since our Return to sovereignty in our Land. But it seems as if God Himself is "lining up the cards" that will bring this sign of the times — the *end* times! — to the attention of Israel and the whole world.

May this gift of life to Jonathan Pollard be just the beginning of wondrous redemption for him and for all those who trust in the Lord.

Richard Upton
And so Jonathan should be set free and incidentally be allowed to live in Israel.I thought Israel and the U.S. were allies.

Sylvia Majetich
Not when it's inconvenient for the US

CHAPTER 19

Jubilee and Disaster

In Chapter 17, we saw that Benjamin Netanyahu held the first-ever Israeli cabinet meeting on the other side of the Jordan River in the Golan Heights, declaring that the Golan will forever be part of Israel.

This was *exactly* the kind of declaration that we would expect to see in a Jubilee year! In an earlier chapter (Chapter 2), we declared that the reunification of Jerusalem as the eternal capital of Israel in 1967 was "amazing," so compared to that, this is merely *notable*. So we shall continue to watch in the coming months to see if God might do something not only *notable*, not only *important*, but *amazing*.

Now we take on a new topic:

Does a Jubilee year signal financial collapse, disaster, or judgment?

We could hardly have chosen a topic that is more highly charged, more subject to hype and ridicule in religious conversation, and yes, even exploitation, especially after the lack of a big market crash last year after the conclusion of the Shemitah year.

First Things First

The very fact we chose to speak on this topic is a clue that, yes, we believe a connection exists. However, do not ignore the fact that we wrote almost 20 chapters on many other Jubilee issues before venturing into this one! Hopefully you will see that delay as a clue to our priorities. However, our comments, although delayed, will not be watered down.

The fact is that Jubilee in Scripture *cannot possibly be divorced from economic implications.* Slaves are set free; debts are forgiven; and the purchase price of land is always proportional to the length of time until the next Jubilee year, when it reverts to its original owner. But, it is equally true that the Jubilee has non-economic elements associated with it. Jubilee embodies freedom throughout the land and the restoration of God's people to their own families! *Such freedom and restoration o families is not just valuable, it is priceless.* Furthermore, in this book, we have tied the Jubilee to spiritual revival, a priceless restoration of people to the family of God.

The S hemitah y ear, a lso c alled t he S abbath y ear, i s s imilar t o the Jubilee. While it comes more frequently, being the seventh year rather than the fiftieth year, it also has both economic and spiritual implications. Our book, *Israel FIRST!*, delves deeply into the Shemitah, looking at both its history and Scriptural principles, economic and spiritual. We then took the risk of making economic and spiritual predictions of what would happen after the Shemitah year ended.

We generally agreed with the conclusions of Jonathan Cahn and his book, *The Mystery of the Shemitah* (Cahn has probably introduced more Christians to the Hebrew word "Shemitah" than anyone else in history!). However, our research led us down a path that caused us to eventually propose some new twists and turns about how the Shemitah would unfold. Our main conclusions include:

1. We believe that if you want to understand how God acts in and around the Shemitah, you must not focus your attention just on the one Shemitah year itself, but on the preceding seven years, and the next seven years. This, by analogy, is like suggesting we should not view the Sabbath as just a day on its own, but as a day that both *ends* the previous week and *leads* us into a new one. This subtle change in perspective makes a huge difference in interpretation, because now we can go to

Scripture and examine how God works in patterns of seven years, not just in the Shemitah year itself. Ultimately, we discovered specific predictions starting with Leviticus 26:14-33 concerning how God reacts to the sin of a nation (such as America) that had previously chosen to walk in His covenant blessings, and proposed that those passages line up with a set of seven-year Shemitah cycles, as detailed in point 3 below.

2. We also emphasized repeatedly that increasing pressure would be brought by God not to simply judge us for its sins, but to *turn* us back to Him, which embodies the very essence of *teshuvah* — repentance.

3. Based on fitting the pattern of Scripture to recent American history, we proposed that Leviticus 26:16 with its phrase, *"I will appoint over you a sudden terror,"* signaled the seven year period beginning with the 9/11 event of September 2001. We then reasoned that Leviticus 26:19 with its phrase, *"I will break down your pride of power"* began the seven-year period beginning October 2008 with its banking collapse, and that this phrase prophesied the loss of respect for America around the world during that seven-year period. Then, based on Leviticus 26:22, we predicted that the seven-year period we just entered in September 2015 would be interpreted with the phrase, *"I will let loose the beasts of the field among you."* **We therefore suggested that a marked increase and a new form of radical Islamic terrorism would begin in Fall 2015, and *not* a financial collapse.** (More on financial collapse below.)

4. Finally, we said the Blood Moons, that were also a source of tremendous foreboding last year, were largely misunderstood. We proposed they should be viewed as a gift from God to the

nation of Israel and not as an omen of impending war. While Syria is wracked with violence, Israel's borders have been a veritable security paradise compared to its neighbors since the beginning of the Blood Moons.

Apologies Offered

Being right about those predictions in no way lessens our sorrow and grief over how the Blood Moons and the Shemitah were used to trade fear for money, essentially monetizing your fear into book, DVD, and product sales. It may sound like we are standing in judgment over other authors, but we actually are not. Despite our best intentions we humbly throw ourselves in with all the other authors as part of the larger problem.

Even though our message was more hopeful than it was dire, who is to say we could not have done a better job ourselves? Might we have done more or worked faster to get the word out about an alternate view of the Blood Moons and Shemitah? We felt overwhelmed by a tidal wave of media coverage like nothing we had ever seen.

So, first if you were fearful in the months leading up to September 2015, or if you were excitedly expecting the Messiah's arrival in those very same months, and then felt misled, confused, and wondering "where is God?" in the relatively calm aftermath of the Blood Moons and the Shemitah year, we two authors want to say to you: **we apologize**.

Second, we apologize for the heavy use of misleading terms such as "market

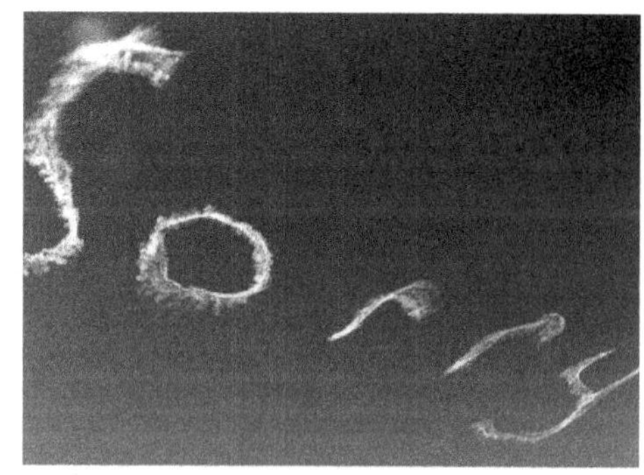

Apology in the sky over Sydney on Australia Day
(Photo: Spud Murphy and Wikicommons)

collapse," "financial collapse," or "market crash," when the proper term that should have been used by everyone is "**market correction**." Market analysts define a market correction as a downturn of more than 20 percent. Not only have we had no crash, but since the peak of the stock market in May 2015, we have not even had a market correction in America. Instead, the market has been "choppy" with several drops less than 20 percent in August and September 2015, and January and February 2016. Each of those times the market bounced back.

Third, we apologize for how many times authors focused your attention on the number of **points** the market dropped, rather than the **percentage**. Focusing on the points alone is like trying to argue that a rancher who owns 100 head of cattle and lost ten of them is worse off than his fellow rancher who only owns 18 heads and lost 9. Clearly the rancher who just lost half his cattle is the one stricken with panic and fear, rather than the one who lost one more cow, but only 10 percent of his assets.

Finally, we apologize for the post-Shemitah articles that redirected your attention to China as a way to **save face** regarding the Shemitah. Yes, it is true that China lost half its stock market value from its peak last June, but what must also be mentioned is that those *losses* were less than the total *gains* in that same year! The China stock market still went up 36% during the Shemitah year, a growth level so strong that the U.S. has only exceeded it once in its last 50 calendar years.

Rest Easy

Now that we have apologized, let us tell you something we find pretty incredible. Even in the midst of all of the chaos before the Shemitah and the relative calm afterwards, you might still have a blessing coming your way without even realizing it. Want to hear more?

Rest area entrance (Photo: Michael Rivera and Wikicommons)

You see, in the midst of all the chaos, a lot of people decided to put some of their finances at rest. Jonathan Cahn for instance — rightly, we think — suggested in August of 2015 that Christians ought to at least consider moving some of their retirement savings from the stock market, going into cash or safer investments. We have heard that many Christians took that advice.

Here is the point: if you took money out of the market and put it into some safer accounts that earned less, but were more predictable, **you just put some of your money at rest**. Why is this at all relevant?

Because like the Shemitah year, the Jubilee year is another Sabbath rest year! As Leviticus 23:11-12 says:

You shall have the fiftieth year as a Jubilee; you shall not sow, nor reap its aftergrowth, nor gather in from its untrimmed vines. For it is a Jubilee; it shall be holy to you. You shall eat its crops out of the field.

As we explain in our book, *Israel FIRST!*, we believe it is important for everyone to make a conscious effort to take a stand against greed. While Jews and Christians outside of Israel are not affected by Israel's Sabbath rest year, it does not prevent them from putting certain activities to rest periodically. Even if you ignore the Shemitah, we argue that it is absolutely mandatory that Christians learn how to stand apart from this world in terms of how to use money. Money must not be our master! The most common way for Christians to stand apart from the world's system is to give liberally to others, but we would also argue that the Bible allows for — and even promotes — the idea of stepping off of the world's highway periodically in an attitude of rest, to stand against the flow of greed that always desires to maximize every investment, and is fearful of missing the next great opportunity for gains. Not only is this beneficial to one's spiritual life, in *Israel FIRST!* we show historical cases of resting investments in Shemitah years that resulted in greater market gains than otherwise.

So, if you let something rest at the end of the last Shemitah year, then, whether you realized it or not, you were also letting that thing rest in the Jubilee Sabbath year, the Jewish year that began on September 14, 2015, and runs through October 2, 2016.

Might God bless you for letting something rest during this current Jubilee year?

Is a Market Correction Coming?

This, then, brings us to the final question of this chapter.

A key insight about the current year has been all but missed in most everything we have seen published.

We are currently in a Shemitah "year" that is TWO years long, because the Jubilee year that follows the Shemitah is a year of rest as well!

Therefore, could some of the financial correction that most people were expecting last year simply be delayed by one more year, in honor of the Jubilee?

Why might God choose to delay serious financial correction until after the Jubilee? Our proposed answer is very simple. A Jubilee is something to which God wants us to anticipate, not dread! While God is adhering to our having entered a new seven-year cycle, which He has indicated by allowing new forms of terrorism, could it be that He would hold back *financial correction* until after this Jewish year ends?

In our earlier book we said that the seven-year cycle we had just entered would probably not start with financial judgment, but that did *not* mean that financial judgment would be missing entirely. Indeed, the very Scripture that we see as applying to this seven-year cycle included (in Leviticus 26:22) the scary phrase *"and destroy your cattle."* We have looked at this from every angle, and do not see any possible way to interpret "cattle" in a way that does not refer somehow to "assets" in some form.

So, if you are trying to honor God by putting your investments at rest right now, we would not advise you to suddenly change course and decide that "the Shemitah is over and all is well." The Shemitah is not over — we are in a last-of-our-lifetime situation for most of us, where the current Shemitah period in which we reside is two years long rather than just one. We might choose to continue the "rest" that we already started.

The world may not notice or care about Jubilee years or the Shemitah, but we cannot stop believing that the Almighty God is watching all. For the sake of His name, He may decide to position certain events in a way that will allow us to look back over time, and see His handiwork.

Is a greater than 20 percent market correction coming in this current seven-year cycle? According to our interpretation of Leviticus 26:22 without repentance, yes!

Do not assume the Shemitah story has ended. It has not. In fact, the real impact of the *end* of the Shemitah year may not even *begin* until the Fall of 2016.

Questions for discussion and thought

Are you putting anything at rest to honor God right now? Your time? Your money? Certain activities?

Another principle of the Jubilee we did not cover above is the aspect of community sharing. This comes from Leviticus 25:11:

You shall eat its crops out of the field.

Jews say this verse should be interpreted as the offering the Shemitah year's harvest to be for the benefit of your local community, rather than being for your personal benefit. Has anyone found an interesting way to model this principle in the current year?

CHAPTER 20

Jubilee and the Return
of the Jewish People to Their Land

This book is coming to its conclusion, and I, Gidon, could not allow that to happen without focusing on what might be the most important aspect of the Jubilee: its relationship to the Jewish people returning to their homeland.

As the foundational verse about Jubilee in Leviticus 25:10 states clearly, the basic point and commandment of Jubilee is the return of land to its original owners:

*You shall thus consecrate the fiftieth year and proclaim **release through the land** to all its inhabitants. It shall be a jubilee for you, and each of you shall **return to his own property**, and each of you shall return to his family.* (emphasis added)

As a Jewish person who has studied Jewish history and is passionate about the incredible story of the revived State of Israel — so much so that I uprooted myself from my nation of birth and even my family to move to this country — it seemed obvious to me that the Jubilee must have significance with regard to the return of the Jewish people, also known as the nation of Israel, to their land, the Land of Israel!

When Bob and I made the decision to write this book, I just knew that I would have to write this chapter. Thank God, the development of the Internet allowed me to research this topic much more quickly than it would take if I would have to travel to libraries and pore through ancient texts.

Surprisingly, however, a Google search resulted in paltry findings, if not downright disappointing. It seemed that any Jewish references to the Jubilee focused on the biblical verses and the rabbinical discussions in the Talmud, but did not go this extra mile to connect the Jubilee to the amazing events unfolding in our very day.

I consulted with the most knowledgeable expert I know on topics related to the End Times in Jewish thought, our very own Root Source teacher Rivkah Adler, who runs a Facebook group called Geula Watch (Geula in Hebrew means redemption, and pretty much parallels the concept of End Times, but usually focusing more on the positive aspects). She encouraged me to post on that page, and I was further disappointed by the low number of responses I got there too.

However, one correspondent on that group named Dov Bar Leib, gave me hope, to say the least. Though he also pleaded ignorance of significant sources on this topic, he referred me to his blog, http:// yearsofawe.blogspot.com/. When I went there, I saw it was a gold mine of information!

I reached out to Dov, and after some divine delays and equally divine help, we met in Jerusalem. Much of what follows here is a small reflection of our discussion that day, which in turn is merely a tiny fraction of the research and ideas he has developed over the past decade. If some of this original research sounds familiar, appearing in previous chapters of this book, I see it as Godly encouragement and acknowledgement of its accuracy.

✡ ✡ ✡

As we have seen, the observance of the Jubilee ceased with the destruction of the Second Temple, around 70 AD. Since then, it has been counted unofficially, according to the different calculation methods described elsewhere in this book: either as an insertion of one year between the forty-ninth year of the previous cycle and the first year of the following one; or as the year following the end of the previous 49-year cycle and simultaneously serving as the first year of the following cycle. (This chapter refers to some dates that seem to fit better with the fifty-year cycle, and some better with the forty-nine-year cycle; none of these references are meant to decide in this question.)

When the Jewish people were exiled from their land after the Second Jewish Commonwealth, as tragic and horrific as that was, many Jews naturally looked back at the First Temple exile, and thought "just as we returned to our Land then with God's help after 70 years, surely this time He will similarly bring us back within a comparable timeframe." And in fact, more or less 70 years after the Temple fell, Bar Kokhba instigated and led the Jewish Revolt, which was seen by many as the Final Redemption, with Bar Kokhba himself filling the role of King Messiah. No less than the greatest Jewish sage of all time, Rabbi Akiva, held this opinion and even acted as Bar Kokhba's arms bearer, until Bar Kokhba died, at which point he was relegated to the category of potential messiahs who died before succeeding completely.

With this Jewish Revolt against the Roman Empire ending in failure, Jewish faith took a turn for the spiritual. Instead of believing that the Regathering of the Exiles would be accomplished by God through His human agents and through their efforts, people started believing more and more that God would bring the Jews back to their land supernaturally, miraculously, with no human effort required besides prayer and following the Torah's commandments. Thus, Jews began "settling in" to their new adopted communities, relegating moving to the Land of Israel as an End Times miracle and viewing life among the nations as the new normal.

But God had other ideas.

While it is beyond the scope of this chapter to explain all the details of the long Jewish exile and why God chose to orchestrate it in the way He did, most Jews are of the opinion that God's countdown clock entered its final finish-line phase in the nineteenth century, only to speed up more and more as the timeline of history approaches its redemptive End Times culmination. See the Root Source channel "Jewish History, Jewish Future" taught by Rabbi Ken Spiro for insights to this.

Why did I write "most Jews" and not "all Jews are of the opinion"? Do not all Jews believe in the coming of the Messiah and the Redemption? Certainly most do; but many are hesitant to recognize this seismic shift in Jewish history. They have become so comfortable in their unnatural state in the exile, that they idealize it to assuage their cognitive dissonance and justify their inaction in response to God's call to return home. They resist assigning divine significance to the State of Israel, with some Jews even seeing it as no less than an affront to God Himself! This partially explains why so many Jews still live everywhere else around the world besides Israel, and even the grotesque phenomenon of ostensibly Orthodox Jews siding with Iran and PLO terrorists.

Throughout the bulk of the last exile, up through the mid-nineteenth century, the Jewish people tried their best to live among their host countries, praying for their governments' well-being as per Jeremiah and *Ethics of the Fathers*:

> *Seek the peace of the city that I have exiled to to and pray for it to God, for in its peace you will find peace.* (Jeremiah 29:7)

> *Rabbi Hanina, Deputy Priest, taught: Pray for the wellbeing of the government, for if not for its authority, people would eat each other alive.* (Ethics of the Fathers 3:2)

But in spite of the Jewish guests' prayer for their host countries, the feeling wasn't mutual, and while Jews were often welcome upon arrival, antisemitism always took over and chased the Jews to another country. A well-known Jewish adage holds (with minor exceptions) that during the exile, no Jewish grandchild was ever buried in the same country that his grandfather was born in.

In parallel with the Jews not being able to put down roots in any of their countries of exile, the Land of Israel lay barren as well. This land, described in the Bible as being of milk and honey, of great lush life and produce, was in "Jewish people exile mode," dry and desert, with no other nation interested and even able to make it prosper. This was prophesied in Leviticus 23:31-32:

I will lay your city in ruins and I will make your sanctuaries desolate…
I will make the land desolate; and your foes who dwell upon it will be
desolate.

Though this sounds like a terrible curse upon the land and the people, Jewish sages explain it in a positive light as well. While the Jews are not in their land, no other people will want or be able to make anything grow in it, so it will be ready for them when they return.

With this in mind, let us review the last four Jubilee years, and see how they act as milestones in God's plans to return the people of Israel to the Land of Israel.

As we mentioned in an earlier chapter, Mark Twain, the pre-eminent writer of his time, visited the Land of Israel and recorded his impressions in his book, *The Innocents Abroad*:

We traversed some miles of desolate country whose soil is rich enough but
is given wholly to weeds — a silent, mournful expanse… A desolation
is here that not even imagination can grace with the pomp of life and

action. We reached Tabor safely... We never saw a human being on the whole route. We pressed on toward the goal of our crusade, renowned Jerusalem. The further we went the hotter the sun got and the more rocky and bare, repulsive and dreary the landscape became... There was hardly a tree or a shrub anywhere. Even the olive and the cactus, those fast friends of a worthless soil, had almost deserted the country. No landscape exists that is more tiresome to the eye than that which bounds the approaches to Jerusalem... Jerusalem is mournful, dreary and lifeless. I would not desire to live here. It is a hopeless, dreary, heartbroken land... Palestine sits in sackcloth and ashes.

This testimony was the harbinger that the Age of Exiles was reaching its end. While pious Jews had been trying to move to the Land of Israel throughout the exile, it was always on an individual basis, with religious motivation, in order to study, pray, and die there. No one was thinking about creating a viable state, with blossoming fields and orchards, the lifeblood of society — self-sustaining food.

No one, that is, until the beginning of the Zionist immigration waves — *Aliyah* — when the Bilu and Hovevei Zion movements inspired over thirty thousand Jews to move to Israel, particularly to establish new agricultural villages there! This development began some 30 years after Mark Twain, the "stranger from a distant land," unconsciously stirred this feeling of Return in the hearts of Jews and Gentiles alike.

Mark Twain wrote this wake-up call for the Jews to return to their Land in 1867 — a Jubilee year.

Between Mark Twain and the First World War, the Jewish population of the land grew from nearly zero to over sixty thousand. This was due to numerous nationalistic and messianic movements, ultimately coalescing into a single political entity — the Zionist Movement. The mission statement of Zionism, founded by Theodore Herzl and still active today, is to establish and maintain re-establishment of a Jewish homeland in the territory defined as the historic Land of Israel. This vision is poetically laid out in what became the State of Israel's national anthem, written in 1877 — 70 years before the state was founded! It was also captured in this prescient statement written by an activist in Israel to his brother in 1882:

> *The ultimate goal ... is, in time, to take over the Land of Israel and to restore to the Jews the political independence they have been deprived of for these two thousand years.*

> *As long as within our hearts*
> *The Jewish soul sings,*
> *As long as forward to the East*
> *To Zion, looks the eye —*
> *Our hope is not yet lost,*
> *It is two thousand years old,*
> *To be a free people in our land*
> *The land of Zion and Jerusalem.*

The Zionists, who only began identifying as such collectively in the late 1890s, and held their first convention in Basel, Switzerland, in 1897, were starting to grow themselves and their land in this embryonic stage, with some 30 new villages being established, among them Tel Aviv. These Zionists celebrated the British conquest of the Ottoman Empire and the Crown's bringing the Holy Land into the twentieth century, especially as it came just months after the Balfour Declaration, a British statement of policy affirming that

> *His Majesty's Government view with favour the establishment in Palestine of a national home for the Jewish people, and will use their best endeavors to facilitate the achievement of this object....*

The Balfour Declaration was issued in 1917 — a Jubilee year.

The history of the period between the Balfour Declaration in 1917, the Partition Plan vote in 1947, and the declaration of Independence of the State of Israel in 1948 is of epic, biblical proportions and is way beyond the scope of this chapter. But in the context of the topic of the Jubilee, it is interesting to quote a well-known entry of Theodore Herzl, the founder of Zionism, in his diary in 1897:

*Were I to sum up the Basel Congress in a word — which I shall guard against pronouncing publicly — it would be this: At Basel I founded the Jewish State. If I said this out loud today l would be greeted by universal laughter. In five years perhaps, and **certainly in fifty years**, everyone will recognize it.* (emphasis added)

Herzl wrote these words in 1897 and predicted the UN resolution founding of the State of Israel in 1947 to the year — a 50-year "jubilee" anniversary!

In fact, the establishment of Israel and its early years were a miracle in the eyes of all who would open theirs to see. But with all the incredible achievements of this nascent nation — and again, to list even a fraction is beyond our scope — it was still in a precarious situation, with the Arab nations surrounding it threatening war from day one (and really from decades beforehand). This menacing threat came to a head on Israel's nineteenth Independence Day, when Egypt deployed troops in Sinai near the border with Israel, and soon thereafter signed a defense pact with Syria and Jordan. The Iraqi army also began deploying troops and armored units in Jordan on Israel's eastern border. The feelings in Israel at the time were best expressed in the gallows humor joke told during those frightening days: "The last one to leave Israel, please don't forget to turn off the lights."

But the lights didn't go out. Israel fought what would be known as the Six-Day War and turned tragedy to victory, including the liberation of Judea and Samaria, the very heartland of biblical Israel.

The Six-Day War was waged in 1967, a Jubilee year.

We have now seen the last three Jubilee years and the astonishing events that coincided with them, from the perspective of Jews returning to their land.

It is furthermore astonishing to note the growth of Jewish population growth in these periods:

- In Mark Twain's time 1867, there were barely 6,000 Jews living in the Land of Israel.

- By the 1917 Balfour Declaration, following the first waves of Zionist immigration, there were 60,000 Jews in the Land.

- Thirty years later and 50 years after Herzl's prophecy, at the time of international recognition of validity of the establishment of Israel in 1947/8, there were 600,000 Jews in Israel.

- By 1967, the year of the liberation of Jerusalem and the biblical heartland, there were 2.5 million Jews in Israel, and approximately 600,000 soldiers in the Israel Defense Forces (IDF).

- Today, 50 years since 1967, there are close to 6 million Jews in Israel, of whom 600,000 live in the greater Jerusalem area, from Geva to Rimon (see Zechariah 14:10). Perhaps unbeknownst to the officials who gave them these names, there is a community just north of Jerusalem named Geva Binyamin, and the southernmost neighborhood of the town of Efrat (adjacent to Bethlehem) is called Rimon.

Recalling the adage mentioned above about grandfathers and grandsons, you can see how the population graph shows a tenfold growth in Jewish population in the Holy Land in our times in every grandfather's and grandchild's generation. Quite a difference from the statistics of the exile....

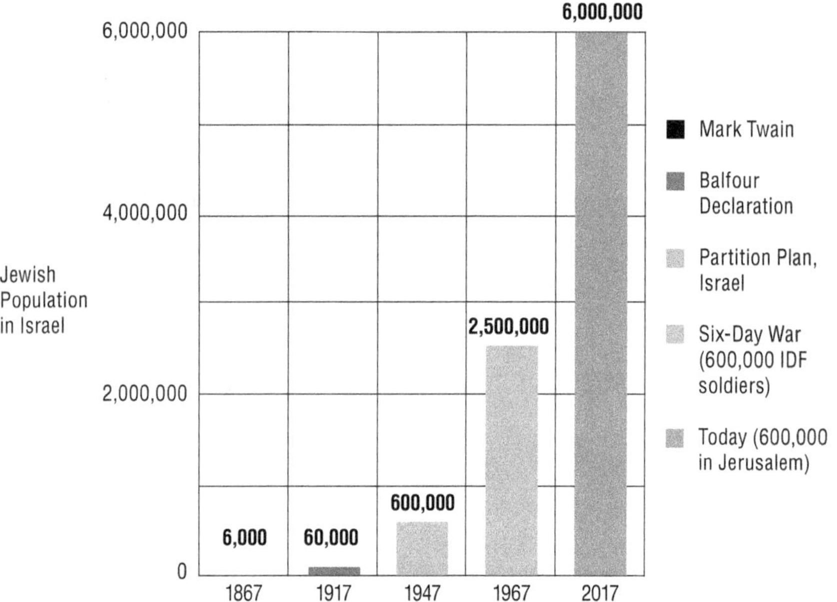

All but 1947/8 fall out on Jubilee years, and it is possible that these population points were triggers for the momentous events they coincided with as well as their Jubilee status. The 1948 population point, arguably the most significant of the years listed, is six hundred thousand, the number listed in the Bible as the population of the people of Israel at the Exodus from Egypt! This brings to mind the awesome prophecies of Micah 7:16: *"As in the days of your exodus from Egypt I will show you wondrous miracles,"* and of Jeremiah 16:14-15:

Therefore, behold, days are coming, says the Lord: and it will not be said God is great and lives, who brought the Children of Israel up and out of Egypt, but rather, God is great and lives, who has brought the Children of Israel up and out of the Land of the North and all of the lands to which he exiled them. And I will return them to their Land, that I gave to their forefathers. (English translations by Gidon Ariel)

What does God have in store for us for this current Jubilee year season?

Watch this progression:

In 1867, God inspired a non-Jew to bring the barrenness of the Holy Land to the attention of the world. While no significant population growth was yet happening in this gestational period, it is worth noting that the first neighborhoods of Jerusalem to be built outside of the city's walls were established around this time as well.

In 1917, that attention by a single non-Jew to the justness of the Jews returning to their homeland was adopted as policy of the leading world empire, and significant population and institution growth began among the Jews in Israel.

In 1947, this policy was adopted by the whole world through its United Nations organization, and Jews attained sovereignty in their land for the first time in nearly 2,000 years.

In 1967, the city of Jerusalem was liberated by the Jewish people, as well as the ancient biblical homeland of the Jews, Judea and Samaria.

What is in store for Israel this year? Could it be the de facto authority of Jordan and the Wakf Islamic religious trust now in place on the Temple Mount finally transferring to the Jewish people? Might even the Third Temple be established? Maybe the biblical borders of Israel promised to Abraham will be inherited by his descendants? Perhaps all these and more, and the final long-awaited Messiah will be revealed, ushering in the concluding era of the Final Redemption?

We dare not frame these hopes and prayers as absolute prophecies. But if you, dear reader, are as fascinated and spellbound as we are about the unfolding of events in our day, we encourage and urge you: continue and increase your good and moral behavior towards your fellows and all of God's children, take a stand against enemies of God and His people, and improve your relationship with the Holy One, Blessed Be He, the God of Abraham.

Or to sum up as Micah exhorted us in chapter 6 verse 8:

[God] has told you, O man, what is good and what the Lord requires of you:

Do justice,
Love kindness,
And walk humbly with your God.

PART II

We now continue the journey to solve the Mystery of the Lost Jubilee!

Part I contains chapters originally published on Breaking Israel News between November 2015 and May 2016.

Part II contains chapters published from May 2016 to March 2018. From this point on, we will state the original date of publication at the beginning of each chapter.

Because this book documents a journey of discovery, we have resisted the urge to rewrite all chapters to bring them up-to-date as if they had all been written after the fact. The journey and what we observed along the way is as important as the final outcome. You can join in the journey, look at the facts as we knew them, and see if you come to the same conclusion we did by book's end. A mystery is still a mystery until the reader reaches the end of the book!

While we did not delete material, we did occasionally add a sentence or two to explain whether a certain prediction turned out to be true.

Part II presents all of the remaining issues surrounding the Jubilee, then heads toward the exciting conclusion and the solving of the mystery.

CHAPTER 21

Adam's Jubilee

NOTE: This chapter was originally written in May 2016.

In Chapter 19, we showed how the Jubilee year is a Sabbath rest, or Shemitah year, and presented the idea that the financial downturn that was expected by so many people in the fall of 2015 might be delayed until the Jubilee year ended in fall 2016. (As of the publishing date of this book in 2018, we now know that Chapter 19 was correct in its prediction that the markets might rest through fall 2016 but was wrong about any possible financial disaster afterwards. Instead, a surprise rally occurred in the markets following the election of Donald Trump in early November 2016. But now let us continue with our story.)

Today, we will look at the very first hint of a Jubilee, and we are going to do that through the life of its very first human, Adam. Not only will you learn the key significance of the number 19 in the life of Adam and in all humankind, but the evidence we find is going to take us in a surprising direction!

Having spent so much time making the case for Jubilees coming every 49 years, we are now going to show that the traditional Jubilee calculation of 50, 100, 150, is also supported in Scripture. So, if you were bothered by all the discussion of 49s, today your 50s ship has come in!

Principle of First Mention

The principle of first mention says that the first mention of any word or topic in Scripture is foundational to its understanding. Chapter 5 of Genesis lists the generations of Adam. Beginning in verse 3 there are successive verses which seem to offer foundational hints to many future patterns in Scripture, including the Jubilee:

> *When Adam had lived one hundred and thirty years, he became the father of a son in his own likeness, according to his image, and named him Seth.* (Genesis 5:3)

First, notice that we are not told when Adam and Eve were forced out of the Garden, nor when Cain and Abel were born. The Book of Jubilees, mentioned in Chapter 16, says that Adam and Eve left at the end of the first seven years after creation, and that Cain and Abel were born between the first and second Jubilee — or between year 49 and year 98.

What God wants us to notice in this verse is the first mention of the word "hundred," the first mention of the word "thirty," and only the second mention of the word "years," which first occurs in Genesis 1:14 as one of the purposes of the sun and moon. We will talk about the number thirty and how it relates to the Jubilee for a future chapter, but we want you to notice here is that the first mention of an age — 130 — is *not* on a Jubilee boundary of either 49 or 50. Because God does not reveal anything in the Bible without a purpose, we can take a lesson from this verse, that God has many varied purposes and plans, and that not all of them are based upon multiples of 7, 49, or 50.

Genesis 5:4 continues:

> *Then the days of Adam after he became the father of Seth were eight hundred years, and he had other sons and daughters.*

Here we have the first use of the word "eight," the number of new beginnings, and 800, the largest number so far mentioned in Scripture.

The stunning point about 800 in this verse however, is that it is on a repeating cycle of 50 years, Adam lived exactly sixteen 50-year Jubilees after Seth was born.

Verse 5 then says:

> *So all the days that Adam lived were nine hundred and thirty years, and he died.*

Here we have the first mention of the number "nine." And this is where a repeating cycle of 49 makes its first showing in Scripture. Because, if Adam lived 930 years, then his life encompassed nineteen 49-year Jubilees: 19 x 49 = 931.

Adam's life ended at a notable boundary. He died in the Sabbatical year of 930, the seventh and final Sabbatical year of the nineteenth Jubilee since creation. Why nineteen? E.W. Bullinger suggests that 19 is the perfection of divine order (9) and judgment (10).

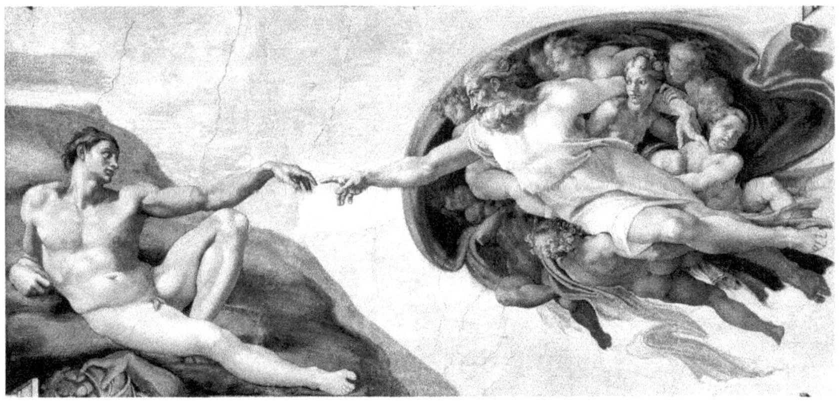

The Creation of Adam, by Michelangelo. (Photo: Public Domain)

Indeed, we see multiple cases of long life, but no human being has ever has reached 20 Jubilees, whether that is measured by 49s or by 50s. Methuselah came the closest at 969 years.

What Scripture Is Saying

The contrast between 800 and 930, and the fact that 800 is mentioned first, gives us some principles we can use in our understanding of the Jubilee going forward.

- We see that the repeating pattern of 50 and 100 is mentioned first. From this we can conclude that such multiples are as important in Scripture as multiples of 49 — even more important. We see this exhibited in Scripture. For instance, God has declared that the Millennium will be 1,000 years long, or twenty 50-year Jubilees. He never said it would be 980 years, as if history's calendar was marked in 49-year increments. Again, God says "a thousand years," not 980 years, "is as one day" (2 Peter 2:9). We must all resist the foolish temptation to fit all of history and its meaning in 49-year cycles. It won't work.

- The repeating pattern of 50 and 100 seems to speak of *generational life shared* together. Adam and Seth enjoyed each other's presence on earth for exactly 800 years. And this not the only such case in Scripture. Enoch lived 300 years after Methuselah. Noah, Shem, and Serug lived 450, 500, and 200 years respectively after the birth of their sons.

Even more notably, Abraham bore Isaac at the age of 100. Then Isaac and his descendants would fulfill God's prophecy that they would live in lands not their own and be mistreated for 400 years until the

Exodus, which occurred 500 years from the birth of Abraham. Indeed, the pattern of 100-year multiples in Scripture is very strong!

Three. Multiple repeating patterns can be like clocks running at the same time, but which are not aligned with each other. We saw that Adam's whole life can be measured in 49-year cycles, but his life with his son is measured in 50-year cycles.

2017 Could Be Important!

How should these ideas affect our thinking?

One conclusion we can reach is that since the Ottoman Turks conquered Jerusalem in 1517, and 400 years later, in 1917, Jerusalem is liberated, 2017 could be a key year in history. *We should take notice,* because these numbers fit the Biblical pattern of the history of Israel. In Chapters 7 and 8, we discussed Judah Ben Samuel's Internet prophecy. The point made in those two chapters was to show we have no proof that Ben Samuel ever prophesied it. But the lack of a Ben Samuel connection in no way invalidates the idea that *the 2017 date could be important.*

Something New?

There's more. The fact that the current Jubilee pattern of 1917 and 1967 fits both a 49- and a 50-year pattern could mean there is a deeper spiritual principle involved, one that we do not fully understand. Perhaps it goes something like this:

Could it be that that individual life is to be lived out in increments of 7 or 49, but generational life is to be lived in increments of 50 or 100? The real answer is probably much deeper. If you have ideas, please share in the comments or email us.

And That's Not All!

Christians have another key reason to watch 2017 that has nothing to do with the Ottoman Turks.

Not only was Jerusalem captured by the Ottoman Empire in 1517, but that year was also the beginning of the Protestant Reformation.

Even more specifically, if we count 400 years exactly from the date that the Protestant Reformation began, October 31, 1517, we reach October 31, 1917. This is the date in which British troops, along with the Australian Light Horse Brigade, captured Beersheba and dealt the mortal blow to the Ottoman Empire's 400-year-long rule of the land of Israel. It would only be a matter of weeks before Jerusalem would be taken by General Edmund Allenby, just as it was taken by the Turks 400 years earlier.

Re-enactment of Australian Light Horse Brigade Charge at Beersheba. (Photo: Public Domain)

One More Thing

And finally, what we notice and find amazing is *the divine convergence* of the 50- and 100-year cycles in the pivotal years of 1917 and 1967 with the 49-year cycles on the Jewish calendar also converging into 1917 and 1967.

Rather than seeing the 49-year cycles and the 50-year cycles as *competing* with each other, and trying to figure out which one is right, the best response is to praise Almighty God for the fact that everything came together like it did in 1917 and 1967.

In the coming days, by watching what happens after October 2016, and by looking at events in 2017 and comparing their differences, we have a unique opportunity in time to more deeply understand the nature of God. Perhaps the meaning of the 49-year cycles and the 50-year cycles will become more clear in the future.

Questions for discussion and thought

Do you have any thoughts about what God might be telling us in the Bible with repeating cycles of 49 (7 x 7) versus repeating cycles of 50 and 100?

CHAPTER 22

6,000 Years Old?

NOTE: This chapter was originally written in June 2016.

In Chapter 21, we showed how Adam's life was exactly nineteen Jubilees long, assuming 49-year-long Jubilees, and that the time he shared with his son Seth was exactly 16 Jubilees long, assuming 50-year-long Jubilees. We suggested that because both kinds of Jubilees were introduced in Scripture together, both interpretations are important, and so we found yet another reason to conclude that the years 2016 and 2017 need to be watched carefully.

In this chapter, we move to Genesis 6 and land on a verse that is now seen as one of the most famous, and briefest, prophecy texts:

> *Then the Lord said, "My Spirit shall not strive with man forever, because he also is flesh; nevertheless his days shall be one hundred and twenty years." (Genesis 6:3 NASB)*

This verse is famous for setting a time limit of human life on earth in the present age — 120 years. In 2016 the "oldest man" was a 112-year-old Israeli Jew, holocaust survivor Israel Kristal. Since this chapter was first written, he has passed away (on August 11, 2017). In 2016 the oldest woman was 116 years old — Emma Morano from Italy. As of February 2018, the oldest man (age 112) and woman (age 117) live in Japan.

120 "Years" of Jubilees

This verse in Genesis, however, has another famous interpretation. This time in the context of the Jubilee sets the lifespan of the earth at 6,000 years. One hundred and twenty Jubilees of 50 years each is exactly 6,000 years: 120 x 50 = 6,000.

The idea that man should reside on the earth for 6,000 years prior to the end of the age was not originally a Christian idea concerning the Messiah's return, but was long woven into Jewish thinking for the Messiah's first arrival. We can see this, for instance, in the Talmud, in tractate Avoda Zara, where we learn that Rabbi Anan passed down from the house of the great prophet Elijah himself that the world was divided into three main periods of time:

- The first 2,000 years were null and void. This was the period of years before the Torah (essentially before Abraham as well).

- The second 2,000 years of the Torah. Approximately from Abraham to the destruction of the second temple.

- The third 2,000 years of the Moshiach. Essentially the period bringing in the Messianic age.

Much discussion in the Talmud and in the commentaries many centuries later has followed from this idea.

At the Rabbi's, by Carl Schleicher.
(Photo: Public Domain)

"A Thousand Years Are Like Yesterday"

In addition to Elijah, a famous verse from Psalms 90:4, combined with the creation story, has led Jews to the same conclusion:

> *For a thousand years in Your sight are like yesterday when it passes by, or as a watch in the night.*

This has caused Jews to write that the total lifespan of the earth is modeled after the 7 days of creation and corresponds to a total of 7,000 years. The first "day" would be Sunday, which lasted 1,000 years, and so on, until the seventh day of rest, which would correspond to the Millennium, or as it is referred to by Jews, the Olam HaBah.

However, this does not mean that the Messiah must arrive exactly at year 6000. Jewish historian Rabbi Ken Spiro points out, "Jewish tradition is that the Messiah must not just arrive by the year 6000, but he must *complete the job* of restoring order to the world by the year 6000."

One Day Equals 1,000 Years

The idea of 6,000 years to the end of the age is also a common belief in Christian literature, not only from the Jubilee calculation, but from the creation week example mentioned above. In fact, the idea that a day should be equivalent to 1,000 years is even plainer in the New Testament than in Psalms. In a passage where the Apostle Peter writes about the great day of judgment at the end of the age he adds this famous statement:

> *But do not let this one fact escape your notice, beloved, that with the Lord one day is like a thousand years, and a thousand years like one day.* (2 Peter 3:8)

He then proceeds to talk about the old earth passing away and a new one coming forth.

Where Are We Now?

While many believe the 6,000-year idea makes sense, the conflict comes when the question is posed: Exactly where in this time frame are we now?

The Jews, through the famous work *Seder Olam*, identify the year 2016 as the 5776th year from Creation, which is still 224 years before the year 6000. Even if the 164 gap years, mentioned in Chapter 16, "Jubilee Across Time," is added, that still leaves us with 60 years to go, before reaching the year 6000. But in either case, given that the Messiah has much work to accomplish, and that work may be started long before it concludes, Jews say it is not too early for him to come now.

Various chronologies have pointed to the millennium year 2000 being at, or close to the 6,000th year since creation. Of course the Messiah did not arrive then. Based on the history of predictions, we can expect that when the Messiah comes, no matter what the year will be, some chronology will have asserted that year to be year 6,000 since creation.

Probably the most well-known Christian chronology has us 20 years beyond 6,000 years already. Developed several hundred years ago, Archbishop James Ussher, had a creation chronology beginning in 4004 BC. Other Christian chronologies count *even more years since creation*, pushing the age of the earth to be more than 6,100 years.

In the Christian view, how could the earth be more than 6,000 years old if the Messiah should return by year 6,000? It would simply mean that God's 6,000 year clock is not always running, in the same way that one widely held evangelical Christian view describes the clock of the Daniel 9 prophecy as currently stopped between the 69th week and the 70th week. One benefit of the proposal that the earth is already more than 6,000 years old is that it can take away the temptation to focus on "date setting" using a countdown.

How Then Shall We Live?

So while opinions differ between Jewish and Christian views, and between individual chronologists, about the age of the earth, most Jews and Christians do agree on one exceedingly important point: ***the Messiah can come any time***.

While this seems like going back to the beginning, throwing out everything we've mentioned, as co-authors, we believe many Jews and Christians can agree on this:

A life well-lived will hold two opposing ideas in continual tension:

- Living with the urgency, desire, and expectation that the Messiah may come very soon, possibly even today. As the Jews pray, "May he come speedily and in our days."

- Living with the long-term view to improve the world in our time, and prepare our great grandchildren to welcome the Messiah long after we ourselves are gone. Jews are taught from their youth the importance of "Tikkun Olam," or repairing the world.

If we individually attempt to hold these two concepts in tension, and if we also work to hold them in tension as a community, we will never be surprised, nor be disappointed, about whether we see the Messiah with our own eyes.

Because each of us has our own biases between the first and second points, we must be willing to live in community with others who have a different view than our own, so that together, as a faith community, we can strive to live harmoniously before God.

May it be so!

Questions for discussion and thought

Do you believe the earth is already more than 6,000 years old?

What does it look like for *you* to live life, holding the two opposing ideas in constant tension? Is it easier for you to be in the first group, or the second?

UK's Jubilee and Brexit

NOTE: This chapter was originally written on June 2016.

In Chapter 22 we discussed the idea of the Earth being about 6,000 years, or 120 Jubilees old. In this chapter, we will discuss the shocking decision by the United Kingdom to exit the European Union.

Britain's exit, or "Brexit" as it is commonly called, caught the world by surprise, as the polls leading up to the June 23rd referendum had the United Kingdom staying in the European Union by a 52 to 48 margin.

Brexit and Jubilee

At first we thought nothing. However, one of our readers, Dennis Northington, was the first to contact us and suggest a connection. He saw this as "The United Kingdom has separated itself from the Nations."

To this we can add that "The United Kingdom is proclaiming freedom throughout the land!"

Now, for those of us not living in the United Kingdom, it might seem like such a statement is bit overreaching. Freedom? Was the UK not already a free democracy? The issue, though, is one of *sovereignty*. About half of the laws being passed in the UK in recent years were forced on them due to their membership in the EU. These regulations were being forced on the UK just like the laws of the federal government of the United States are forced on the States. But unlike the federal government in the US, the people of the UK did not elect the officials who were making those decisions.

The UK did not exit the European Union because they knew that it is better for them economically. They have exited the European Union as a matter of sovereignty, of freedom.

The Timing

The Brexit vote occurred in the middle of the Jewish year we have been watching for signs of Jubilee. The Brexit follows just two months after the declaration by Israel that Golan shall be forever part of Israel — also in this Jubilee year.

But, is there any connection with the European Union to Jubilee years of the past?

The formation of the European Union, named as such, is traced back to the Maastricht Treaty which went into force on November 1, 1993, a Shemitah year. However, some have said the original formation of the European Union dates back to the formation of the European Communities in the Merger Treaty, or Brussels Treaty, that became effective on July 1, 1967. This is less than a month after the Reunification of Jerusalem in 1967, which this book has often suggested as being a Jubilee year!

The European Union — Good or Bad for the World?

Much has been written about the spiritual implications of the formation European Union and its role in propagating a one-world government and fulfilling End-Times prophecy.

European Union Flag
(Wikicommons)

While there is no reason to repeat all that here, we call our readers' attention to a point made by Paul McGuire and Troy Anderson in their book *The Babylon Code.* They note that the official anthem of the European Union, *Ode to Joy,* calls forth a vision of a one-world government devoid of Almighty God. The first verse explains it:

> *Joy, beautiful spark of divinity,*
> *Daughter from Elysium,*
> *We enter, drunk with fire,*
> *Heavenly, thy sanctuary!*
> *Your magics join again*
> *What custom strictly divided;*
> *All people become brothers,*
> *Where your gentle wing abides.*

It seems to us that this decision by the UK, which we hope will be followed by other EU member countries, is a decision to chart its own course, giving the country the freedom, and therefore the possibility, to follow a path ordained by God.

Is this a new beginning in a Jubilee year for the United Kingdom? Let us all pray that many in the UK choose to follow God fully in the next 50 years. And all along the way, "Let freedom ring!"

174

Questions for discussion and thought

Do you see the Brexit as a key Jubilee-year event?

CHAPTER 24

Let's Be Civil

NOTE: This chapter was originally published June 30, 2017.

In Chapter 23, we discussed the United Kingdom's exit from the European Union as a key Jubilee event in its history. Now, we move on from Genesis to Exodus 12:1–2 and arrive at verses that raise a fundamental question about the Jewish calendar, and therefore the Jubilee year. When God instituted the Passover, He introduced it this way:

> *Now the Lord spoke to Moses and Aaron in the land of Egypt, saying, "This month shall be your beginning of months; it shall be the first month of the year to you."* (NKJV)

The month discussed in these verses is the month in which Passover occurs, the month of Nissan, which begins in the spring.

Then why does the Jewish year, and therefore the Jubilee year, begin in fall and not spring?

Be Biblical in Spring, But Be Civil in Fall

This simple question has caused much confusion. Even today Jews understand that there are multiple "beginnings" to the year, and they consider that while the Biblical New Year occurs in spring on the first day of Nissan, the standard Jewish calendar, a civil calendar, currently in the year 5776, begins on the first day of Tishrei in the fall, a day generally referred to as Rosh Hashana. This phrase literally mean "the head of the year."

In this chapter, we will consider why the Jubilee year begins in the fall, and in the next chapter we will consider why the Jubilee begins on the tenth day of the month, rather than the first day.

To help us understand these things, we met with Rabbi Yoel Bin Nun, who has published an article on the Jubilee that helped us resolve much confusion on these topics.

Rabbi Bin Nun says that while the Torah is explicit that the year begins in spring, it also contains verses which state that the year ends and begins in fall. For instance:

Rabbi Yoel Bin Nun. (Photo by Bob O'Dell)

> *And the festival of the harvest, the firstfruits of your labors, which you have sown in the field, and the festival of the ingathering,* **at the end of the year***, when you gather in your labors from the field.* (Leviticus 23:16)

> *And you shall observe the festival of weeks, of the first fruits of the wheat harvest, and the festival of the ingathering,* **at the end of the year**. (Leviticus 34:22)

> *At the* **end** *of every seven years, at the time of the year of the Shemitah, on the festival of Sukkot....* (Deuteronomy 31:10)

So clearly, as the Rabbi explains, there are two beginnings to the year in the Torah.

But why should the counting of the years begin in the fall, and not the spring? To answer this question Rabbi Bin Nun refers us to the verses:

*So long as the earth remains — **sowing time and reaping time, and cold and heat, and summer and winter**, and day and night, will not cease.* (Genesis 8:22)

Now consider a key verse regarding the counting of years:

*And for six years shall you **sow** your land and **gather** in its produce, But the seventh year you shall let it rest and lie fallow, that the poor of your people may eat.* (Leviticus 23:10-11)

By connecting these two verses, the implication is quite clear that the counting of years is to begin in the time of sowing, which is in the fall.

Those of us who live in cities and are not as connected to the agricultural cycles may not realize the importance of fall as the primary ingathering. But as the diagram shows, the ingathering is a process that begins with the barley harvest, continues over the summer, and concludes in the fall.

Harvesting and Ingathering in Israel

	Mar	Apr	May	Jun	Jul	Aug	Sep	Oct	Nov
Barley		✡							
Peas		✡	✡						
Wheat			✡						
Lentils		✡	✡						
Vetch		✡	✡						
Oats			✡						
Sesame					✡				
Flax					✡				

	Mar	Apr	May	Jun	Jul	Aug	Sep	Oct	Nov
Millet					✡	✡			
Grapes				✡	✡	✡	✡		
Figs						✡	✡		
Pomegranates						✡	✡		
Olives							✡	✡	✡

Source: Israel Ministry of Agriculture

For Rabbi Bin Nun, the real question is not whether there is a beginning to the year in the fall, but exactly when does it begin? The phrase "Rosh Hashana" does not occur in the Bible. The first day of Tishrei is only referred to in the Bible by its other name, "the day of the shofar blast" or Yom Teruah.

So why is the first day of Tishri referred to as Rosh Hashana, when the Scriptures are so vague on the topic? And why would the Jubilee year begin on the tenth day of that same month rather than the first day of the month? That is will be the subject of our next chapter.

Questions for discussion and thought

Why do you think God created two calendars to run concurrently — one that begins in the spring and one that begins in the fall?

(If you need a hint, consider why God allowed history to be told twice: not only in Kings, but also in Chronicles.)

CHAPTER 25

Why the Tenth Day?

NOTE: This chapter was originally published July 2017.

In Chapter 24, we showed the biblical basis for the Jubilee year to begin in fall, even though God told the Israelites that the religious calendar begins in spring. But as we move from Exodus into Leviticus we discover find an emphatic statement from God that the Jubilee year does not begin on the first day of the month, but the *tenth* day of the month:

> *You shall then sound a ram's horn abroad on the tenth day of the seventh month; on the day of atonement you shall sound a horn all through your land. You shall thus consecrate the fiftieth year and proclaim a release through the land to all its inhabitants.* (Leviticus 25:9–10 NASB)

Because the release is proclaimed on Yom Kippur, the Day of Atonement, which is the tenth day of the month, it is widely regarded that the Jubilee year only begins on this tenth day. This seems to make the Jubilee unique among years in that the civil new year in every other Jewish year begins on the first day of the seventh month, also known as Rosh Hashana.

This creates an obvious problem in the Jewish calendar. Do you see it? If the previous year *begins and ends* on Rosh Hashana, but the Jubilee year only begins on Yom Kippur, then for the 10 days before

Jubilee begins, the Jews live in a time gap in which they have no year at all! Similarly if the Jubilee year *lasts a full year,* then the last 10 days of the Jubilee year create a time overlap with the first 10 days of the succeeding year, making the Jews unsure about which year they are living in during those 10 days.

Time to Wake Up!

The answer to the dilemma, in our opinion, is once again found in the writings of Rabbi Yoel Bin Nun, whom we referenced in the last chapter. When we read his opinion on this topic, not only did we find an answer to the Jubilee time gap, but we learned something about the nature of God, man, and time that might just change that way you view the Jewish calendar, and even all time.

Our view of time in the Western world is shaped by the Greek mindset of classification that approaches complexity by breaking complex topics down into individual components and classifying them. In this thinking, for example, an automobile is understood by looking at all of its component parts and how they work. A year is understood by looking at units of time — days, hours, minutes and seconds, etc. — and how they are organized. And by extension of that organization, one year transitions to another year at exactly 12 midnight on December 31st. The transition is instantaneous, so than any "moment" is classified as belonging to one year or the next.

Happy New Year
(Wikicommons)

'Tis the Season

Now going back to the Jewish calendar, this apparent conflict in the Jewish calendar (between the first day and the tenth day of the seventh month concerning which will be the start of the year), caused Rabbi Bin Nun to ponder and propose a very different idea: "Suppose that the 'start of the year,' the 'Rosh Hashana' in the Torah, was not meant to actually refer to a single *day* at all, but rather a *season*, one that begins with Rosh Hashana on the first day of the month, and ends on the very last day of Sukkot, the 21st day of the month."

In this view, the sounding of the trumpet on Rosh Hashana on the first day of the seventh month is not the start of a new year, but announces the *beginning of the month in which the new year begins, and therefore also the beginning of the month in which the previous year also ends.*

Rabbi Bin Nun noticed that if that view is taken, many problems and contradictions suddenly disappear:

- It explains why the Torah never refers to the first day of the seventh month as the day of the new year (Rosh Hashana), but it only refers to that day as Yom Teruah, the Day of Trumpeting.

- It explains how a Jubilee year can have multiple starting points — both the first day of the month and the tenth day of the month.

- It explains why the Torah sometimes refers to the beginning of the year as the time of sowing, and sometimes as occurring after Sukkot.

- It explains why no elaborate feast is ever celebrated on the first day of any month, and even Yom Teruah is described *only* as a time of blowing the trumpets.

- It explains why Yom Kippur, the Day of Atonement, is a day to forgive sins of the previous year.

- It helps reconcile the idea that the agricultural new year and the rains that go with it begin only after the festival season is completed.

Poetry in Motion

Rabbi Bin Nun elaborates on this view of time in the following way:

> *The perception of time in the Torah particularly, and in the world of religious thought in general, is not linear and detached. It is inconceivable, from this perspective, to circle specific dates in an office diary, or to tear off pages with days which have gone by. The religious view of time is built on a consciousness of continuity, cyclical repetition, and remembrance.*
>
> *In a continuous consciousness, no day stands alone; it is always connected with the previous day and the following day in a chain of successive links.... They are part of a chain that connects them to periods that have already come and gone, and especially to the parallel period last year and in previous years. They also look into the mists of the period that is to come, and of future years.*
>
> *This consciousness is also inseparably bound up with the cyclical order of nature. Every season in nature is accompanied by its own special feelings, appearance, and familiar smell of sunsets and sunrises; days growing shorter or longer, alternations of heat and cold, humidity and dryness, sowing and reaping. This is in nature "a remembrance of the act of Creation."*

Beginning of the End, and End of the Beginning

Rabbi Bin Nun uses the transition from one day to the next as a way to visualize these ideas. The end and beginning of a new day occurs at sunset in the Hebrew calendar, but the transition is not instantaneous. The twilight of the previous day is still gloriously present on the western horizon as the new day begins. In this view of time we can see that "the period of twilight belongs to both days." It is for this very reason that in the Jewish view, the Shabbat day lasts 25 hours rather than 24. "We hurry to bring it in and take our time parting from it," says the Rabbi.

Twilight over West Jerusalem. (Photo: Bob O'Dell)

The same thought applies to the agricultural cycle, where it is possible to be sowing and reaping at the same time, as described in Amos 9:13:

> *Behold the days are coming when the plowman will overtake the reaper, and the treader of grapes will overtake him who sows the seeds.*

The season of days that marks the beginning and the ending of a year, both a standard year and Jubilee, is marked by a period that simultaneously belongs to the preceding year and the following year, just as the links of a chain touch each other.

Coincidently, the 10 days between Rosh Hashana and Yom Kippur also fit nicely inside the 11-day difference between the 365-day solar year and the typical 354-day lunar year, showing that God designed the orbits of the earth and moon to correspond to his invention of the new year festivals. The difference between the calendar from one year to the next is accounted in time, meaning that Yom Kippur of the second year, is very nearly the time of Rosh Hashana on the preceding year, creating "links in time" from year to year.

Implications of This Idea

The implications of Rabbi Bin Nun's ideas when extended further could be enormous. extending well beyond the topic of the Jubilee. In Rabbi Bin Nun's way of perceiving time, the rebirth of Israel as a nation is not to be seen *only* as having happened on May 14, 1948, a nation born in a day, but also as a process, a transition in time taking many years. Similarly, the rebirth of Jerusalem must not only be seen as an event in June 1967, but as a season, one that might have lasted an entire 49- or 50-year Jubilee cycle in its length!

As we move into 2017, we arrive upon the date of the 50-year anniversary of the reunification of Jerusalem and the date of the 70-year mark since the world, through the United Nations, agreed to create a Jewish state in 1947. We could view ourselves as not simply reaching an anniversary, but reaching "the period of the end of the beginning" of the birth of Israel as a nation. And what of the future? Might we also be seeing the beginning of the next phase in the life of the nation? Might this be the long-term implication of Benjamin Netanyahu's statement on March 3, 2015, before the United States Congress when he declared that "even if Israel has to stand alone, Israel will stand."

This idea of time also explains beautifully why a Jubilee year can be a year that births an idea that can take years or decades to fully develop, such as what we may have witnessed in the referendum in United Kingdom to chart a new course for itself outside of the European Union. That vote was a "decision to leave" while the process of leaving will take months and years.

Finally, Rabbi Bin Nun's idea brings illumination to the New Testament ideas that simultaneously say that while the season may be known, the day and hour will not be known by anyone.

Questions for discussion and thought

Does the view of time presented in this article resonate with you? Why or why not?

How might this affect your view of a "changing of a season" in your life?

CHAPTER 26

The Ninth of Av

NOTE: This chapter was originally written in August 2016.

In Chapter 25, we showed that the end of a year in God's calendar is not an instantaneous event, like December 31st at midnight, but stretches over a period of days, beginning with Rosh Hashana and ending with the blowing of the shofars on Yom Kippur.

In this journey of discovery, we have usually waited for events to happen, watched what God was doing, and then written about those events. These included, for example, the declaration of a Jubilee Year by Pope Francis and the declaration of Golan forever being part of Israel by the Prime Minister of Israel. In this chapter, we are writing about the Ninth of Av before it happens.

The day on the Jewish calendar that is commonly referred to in English as the Ninth of Av is called Tisha B'Av in Hebrew, literally meaning "ninth in Av." Av is the fifth month of the biblical calendar that starts in spring with the month of Nissan and the eleventh month of the civil calendar that began the Jubilee year last fall in the month of Tishri.

Tragedy of Tragedies

This day is both famous and infamous in Jewish history as the day on which more trouble has occurred for the Jewish people than any other day. On the Gregorian calendar, this day falls either in July or August, but the remarkable series of events that have occurred on this day throughout history is beyond any random coincidence.

- It was on this day that the spies reported back to the Israelite people that the land of Canaan was too difficult to conquer. This negative report delayed the entry into the Promised Land by 40 years.

- It was the exact day of the destruction of the First Temple built by Solomon.

- It was the exact day of the destruction of the Second Temple in the 1st Century.

- It was the exact day of the crushing of the Bar Kochba revolt in the 2nd Century.

- It marked the expulsion of Jews from England in 1290 CE.

- It marked the first day of the absence of Jews in Spain after they were expelled in 1492 CE.

- It marked the day of the start of World War I, which is seen as the beginning of the sequence of events that led to the Holocaust during World War II.

Fasting and Praying on Ninth of Av

Today Jews abstain from food and water on this day, to physically identify with the suffering of the history of the Jews. They begin preparing for this event three weeks in advance, on the 17th day of Tammuz, the month prior to Av, which marks the day that Nebuchadnezzar's Babylonian army breached the walls of Jerusalem three weeks before the destruction of the First Temple.

Second Temple Destruction on Tisha B'Av, by Francesco Hayez. (Photo: Wikicommons)

After the return of the Jewish people to the land after the Babylonian exile, they completed the building of the Second Temple. The prophet Zechariah records in chapter 7 of his book that the Jews asked if they should continue to be sorrowful on each Ninth of Av, in commemoration of the destruction of the First Temple, now that a Second Temple was standing in its place. The prophet Zechariah answered yes, do not cease being sorrowful, but look towards the future, as recorded in Zechariah 8:18–19:

> *Then the word of the Lord of hosts came to me, saying, "Thus says the Lord of hosts, 'The fast of the fourth, the fast of the fifth, the fast of the seventh and the fast of the tenth months will become joy, gladness, and cheerful feasts for the house of Judah; so love truth and peace.'"*

The fast of the fourth month is the 17th day of Tammuz mentioned earlier. The fast on the fifth month is the Ninth of Av, falling on Sunday, August 14th in 2016. The fast on the seventh month is the Fast of Gedaliah (next occurring on October 5, 2016), and the fast on the tenth month was already held this past winter.

The prayer on the Ninth of Av is not just one of expressing sorrow for the past loss, but it is also a prayer for the future, that God would hasten and bring in the promise of Zechariah 8.

For more details on how these fasts are observed, we refer you to a video by Gidon Ariel: root-source.com/blog/tisha-beav-day-of-calamity-prayer-for-redemption.

An Invitation to Join with Jews in Prayer

We would like to take this opportunity to invite Christians to join together with the Jewish people in prayer, as we pray each year:

May this be the year that this day of sorrow will be turned into joy and redemption for the Jewish people.

Gidon Ariel by the Walls of Jerusalem. (Photo: Bob O'Dell)

The link mentioned previously gives background and information about how you might pray with us. Some Christians may desire to fast on that day as well. You are welcome to join in any part of our fast, but please do so only if you can do it safely and responsibly.

The Importance of Joining

There is a context for joining in observing the Ninth of Av this particular year as it relates to the Jubilee.

The good news is that in all of Jewish history, none of the Ninth of Av tragedies mentioned earlier seems to have fallen on a Jubilee year. Last year's Ninth of Av in the Shemitah year was also relatively free from trouble in Israel.

But it seems to us that the nation collectively "holds its breath" each year on this day, wondering if another tragedy may befall it. So the first reason to participate is because of brotherly love.

The second reason to join in this particular year is in the context of the Jubilee year. It is rare for any great gains in land to occur without conflict. If God were to do something amazing in this Jubilee year, as He did in 1967, it may well be associated with conflict, even though we have repeatedly prayed that such would not happen.

The third reason to join in praying with Jews in this particular year is that some notable Christian prophecies have spoken about war or conflict coming to the land of Israel soon. If such conflict were to come in Jewish year 5776, the current Jewish year, then the Ninth of Av would be a prime day for it to begin.

The fourth and final reason to join in praying with Jews this year is that since we may well be in a Jubilee year right now. *This is the start of a new cycle.* That passage in Zechariah 8 continues with a prophecy that involves all peoples, not just the Jews. As you read it, consider this year as an opportunity to *begin something new*, a new way of walking with the Jewish people. Zechariah 8:20–21 says:

> *Thus says the Lord of hosts, "It will yet be that peoples will come, even the inhabitants of many cities. The inhabitants of one will go to another, saying, 'Let us go at once to entreat the favor of the Lord, and to seek the Lord of hosts; I will also go.'"*

Who is to say that this fulfillment can begin only when the Ninth of Av becomes a day of joy? Why can't we, who are non-Jews, begin to fulfill this verse on Sunday, August 14, 2016?

Questions for discussion and thought

The Ninth of Av on August 14, 2016, turned out to be trouble-free. But, regardless of when you read this chapter, would you consider Gidon's invitation to join the Jews in prayer and/or fasting at the next Ninth of Av?

2018 - July 22

2019 - August 11

2020 - July 30

2021 - July 18

2022 - August 7

Consult hebcal.com for other dates.

The Year of the Lord's Favor

NOTE: This chapter was originally written in August 2016.

In the last chapter, we examined the Ninth of Av, the quintessential day of tragedy for the Jewish people, and we invited Christians to join with Jews in prayer on that day.

Following that darker topic let us examine a very bright one:

Is Jubilee in general, and perhaps this year in particular, the Year of the Lord's Favor?

Many have commented publicly as well as written to us privately about the potential connection of the Jubilee with Isaiah 61:1–2:

The Spirit of the Lord God is upon me, because the Lord has anointed me to bring good news to the afflicted; he has sent me to bind up the brokenhearted, **to proclaim liberty to the captives** *and freedom to prisoners;* **to proclaim the favorable year of the Lord....*"

Regarding this passage and its Messianic message, Christians additionally point out that these phrases were also quoted by Jesus. But putting that aside, both Jews and Christians do agree fully that this Isaiah 61 passage is Messianic in nature.

It is the phrase "to proclaim liberty to the captives" which has traditionally connected this verse to the Jubilee since the foundational passage on Jubilee in Leviticus 25:10 uses a similar term:

> *You shall thus consecrate the fiftieth year and* **proclaim a release** *through the land to all its inhabitants....*

The word "release" in Leviticus and the word "liberty" in Isaiah are the same Hebrew word, *deror*, which can be translated release, liberty, a flowing, free run, and even freedom.

Freely Flowing Water.
(Photo: Sherwood Burton)

Jubilee as the Year of the Lord's Favor: Yes or No?

So on the face of it, we can see the obvious connection in Isaiah 61 with the Jubilee year, since the Jubilee-type phrase "proclaim a release" (*deror*), is followed almost immediately in Isaiah 61 by a proclamation of the "year of the Lord's favor."

The "Yes camp" seems ready to gain a quick victory.

But, here is where the problems begin, and the "No camp" gains some ground. First, the word "favor" (Hebrew: *ratson*) in Isaiah 61 is not used in Leviticus 25. Second, the "year of favor" in Isaiah 61:2 is followed immediately by the phrases   "... and the day of *vengeance* of our God; to *comfort* all who mourn."

Most Christians do push those last two phrases into the future since they were specifically omitted by Jesus in his list of those prophecies which he was fulfilling at the time. The point we as authors are attempting to make here is that this Messianic passage *has elements* which seem to go beyond the Jubilee as described in Leviticus, i.e., vengeance and comfort.

On the other hand, the past Jubilee years of 1967 and 1917 contained full-fledged wars, as we previously discussed. Honest soldiers in the ranks of the Ottoman Turks in 1917, on the side of the Arab nations surrounding Israel, might well have felt that God was bringing a kind of "divine vengeance" upon them. The strategies of those armies clearly backfired. Putting this observation in the context of biblical times, the first year the children of Israel entered into the land of Canaan definitely had Jubilee aspects to it: the returning of the Promised Land to Israel, a divine vengeance upon the city of Jericho, and the need for comfort after the tragic engagement by Israel in the battle for the next city to be conquered, Ai.

Jewish Hints

A few more hints on this topic come from Jewish perspectives.

First of all, Jews pray every day for the current year to be a blessed and fruitful one. They ask God to bless all the produce of the land, and they begin to pray for rain immediately after the Sukkot holiday ends, and it often rains on cue. So their prayer is that every year would be blessed. (Jewish prayers for rain were answered in Jerusalem right after Sukkot in 2016, and just following the day of the water libation during Sukkot in 2017.)

Second, in the description of Jubilee in Leviticus 25:21, the reader might notice that it is actually the 48th year and not the Jubilee year that is to be the most fruitful of all, carrying a blessing into the Sabbatical year and the Jubilee year that follows it:

> *I will so order My blessing for you in the **sixth year** that it will bring forth the crop for three years.*

The Key to an Answer

So how do we resolve the question: Is the Jubilee — and Jewish year 5776 — the Favorable Year of the Lord? (Reminder that this question was being asked in August 2016.)

The key to resolving the question is to notice *who is responsible* to proclaim liberty in these two passages.

In God's commands to Israel as set out in Leviticus 25, the decision to enact a Jubilee is a responsibility of the people! Unless everyone joins together in accepting that liberty shall be proclaimed, nothing will happen. And further, the cooperation on actions to be taken in the 50th year must begin in the very first year of that cycle, because the economic system — the value of land and one's service — is to be proportional to the number of years that remain until the Jubilee, when the land is returned and slaves are set free. In other words, the timing and coordination of the 50th year has to be known and agreed to by everyone a full 50 years in advance!

Yet in Isaiah 61, the decision to proclaim a release and to declare the favorable year of the Lord is the responsibility of the Messiah! This elegant redemption is under His authority. As such, it need not happen on cue once every 49 or 50 years. **It can happen anytime**!

Bob would like to point out to Christian readers that Jesus quoting Isaiah 61 in Luke 4 in approximately 29/30 AD does not seem to be in a Jubilee year. If you start with the year 1967 and walk back in a 49-year repeating pattern, you come to 7 AD. If you walk back in a 50-year repeating pattern, and you get to 17 AD. Neither of these years is very close to 29 AD, but the good news here is that, by extension, the Messiah's imminent arrival can come in any year as well!

Now with this "who is responsible" distinction in mind, we can now look back and see that the root of the principle of Messianic redemption is even present in Leviticus 25. Apart from a few exceptions, this chapter goes to great lengths to explain how the land and people can be redeemed *at any time* by kinsmen. This is how Boaz claimed Ruth.

The idea that the favorable year can be both "known in advance," and "happen any time" is actually the most exciting answer to the question that we could imagine! Why? First, because, as we have said before, there is no definitive evidence that the Jubilee principles were ever practiced on a national level by Israel. If a year of the Lord's favor requires an entire nation to come together 50 years in advance and agree to enact something as unusual, tumultuous, and upending as the

Jubilee over the next 50 years, it might never happen. But if, as Isaiah proclaims, the Messiah is not bound by the laws of the Jubilee, then the Messiah *is willing* to do the difficult work that we could not make happen within our community on earth.

Why Bother?

So if the Messiah will declare a Messianic Jubilee in his own timing, then why do we bother to search for and solve the Mystery of the Lost Jubilee at all?

Finding the Lost Jubilee and participating in it is not going to solve every problem. The Jubilee year does not guarantee every prayer to be answered in the way we desire. But we believe that when man attempts to honor God, recognize God's principles, and take a few feeble steps to participate in what God might be doing, that act pleases Him. For the nation of Israel, those steps can result in more of the Promised Land being returned. Furthermore, when God does something beautiful for the Jewish people in the land of Israel, He often does something beautiful for the nations of the world as well.

Questions for discussion and thought

If the Messiah has the authority to declare a Jubilee at any time, what Jubilee-like change in your personal, family, or community situation would you most like to see happen?

CHAPTER 28

Finally Found?

NOTE: This chapter was originally written on November 10, 2016.

In this book we have looked at the Jubilee year from both Jewish and Christian perspectives to examine whether God might be restoring the Jubilee calendar as described in Leviticus 25.

This article examines whether recent "upset events" like Trump's win and the Brexit can help us identify whether a Jubilee is here.

Remember, Jubilee is the largest systematic social reconstruction tool in the Bible, short of the inauguration of Messianic rule at the end of the age. It is a divine reset of the land every 50 years that gives the poorest of the land a chance to restart their lives in a new direction. Slaves are set free. People who have sold, given away, and even been tricked out of their most precious possession — their own land — get it back.

In the economies of ancient times, it was not God's, but man's, "golden rule" that always prevailed: Those who have the gold make the rules. Thus the rich and powerful made sure that they could stay that way (short of a populist revolt), and the poor were managed and frequently abused by their rulers in a way that would skew ever more of the available resources to those at the top.

The Jubilee was God's invention to systematically and periodically uproot this human tendency, giving every family of the earth the chance, at least once in their lifetime, to be part of a grand reset: to move in a new direction and gain economic success.

Reset Icon (Wikicommons)

In this book, we have asked whether God might be in the process of restoring the Jubilee to the world. That process, we reasoned, should begin by restoring the Jubilee calendar itself. Indeed, there seems to be a striking pattern exhibited through a series of key events that have occurred in 50-year cycles, most notably relating to the nation of Israel, but even extending to the rest of the world. We have pointed out that pattern of events in late 1917, such as the Balfour Declaration and the retaking of Jerusalem by the British, and the events in the spring of 1967, such as the Six Day War and the Reunification of Jerusalem. These events were so startling that we suggested we must watch the events of 2016/2017 to see whether God might do something important in the nation of Israel. On the Hebrew Calendar, we would first examine the Jewish year of 5776 (roughly September 2015 through October 2016), and on the Gregorian calendar, we will watch through the end of 2017.

This chapter looks at the evidence for a Jubilee year ending in 5776, a year that is now fully in the books.

Has there been clear evidence of Jubilee-like events in the year of 5776 in Israel?

Our view is that everything begins with Israel, so we must look there first.

There has been one big decision occurring in the nation of Israel that is Jubilee-like in that it relates to the restoration of land to the Jewish people. On Sunday April 17, 2016, as mentioned in Chapter 17, Prime Minister Benjamin Netanyahu took his cabinet across the Jordan River to the Golan Heights and declared that the future status of the Golan Heights had been irrevocably decided: the Golan will be forever part of Israel. He went on to say that the Golan is now to Israel what Jerusalem is to Israel.

Golan Heights seen from the Sea of Galilee. (Photo: Bill Sellstrom)

While we desired to see Jews become completely free to pray on the Temple Mount (which did not happen), the change in status in the Golan was the most notable shift of its kind since 1967. This is the first time that the nation of Israel has formally annexed land on the eastern side of the River Jordan in its modern history! It is the number one reason why 5776 can be considered a Jubilee year.

Has there been any clear evidence of Jubilee-like events in the year of 5776 in the world at large?

The Brexit vote in the United Kingdom on June 23, 2016 (described in Chapter 23) fits the Jubilee pattern. It seems appropriate that the same nation that helped propel the establishment of a Jewish homeland in 1917 should itself be set free from the clutches of the European Union in the Hebrew calendar year of 5776. The separation of Britain from the EU was also coupled with the change of power and the appointment of Theresa May as Britain's prime minister, a pro-Israel one at that. The UK is now free to chart its own course in the years ahead.

What was notable about this Brexit referendum was the populist nature of the vote — giving hope to the working class and standing against globalism. This provision of hope for the downtrodden, coupled with freedom to choose one's own path forward, is very much the theme of Jubilee.

What about other key elections around the world?

Two other election "upsets" have recently rocked the world, one before, and another just after the year 5776.

In March 2015, Benjamin Netanyahu and the Likud party shocked Israel and the world by winning a landslide victory. Many see this as not just an election, but the end of an era, the era of two-state solution proposals. Israel's demographics are changing to favor a more conservative and religious political view. This vote was an instance of

President Donald Trump
(Photo: Wikicommons)

the people speaking. While this election was actually in year 5775, it seems to have been a harbinger of the future upsets that were upcoming, such as the Brexit in 5776, and now the Trump victory in early 5777 on November 8th.

America's election in November 2016 made Trump an upset winner. Like Brexit, this populist decision, the most dramatic upset in more than one hundred years in the US, is once again reminiscent of the Jubilee — a desire for freedom from government as we know it.

Jubilee as a Year of Rest — What else has happened?

The Jubilee is not just about slaves being set free and land being returned, it is about rest.

The year 5776 was one of the most watched years ever with respect to war against Israel. The prevailing view was that the Blood Moons and Shemitah years could signal a war against Israel in 5776 — a view we have always opposed. We found no basis for that claim in Scripture nor in history. In our book *Israel FIRST!*, we stood against the tide and predicted God's blessing on Israel in the post–Blood Moons period, even though we held our breath a bit regarding the signing of the Iran deal in late 5775 (summer 2015).

Instead, what we saw was God's grace was upon Israel in 5776. Israel's relationship with Jordan, Egypt, and even Turkey and Saudi Arabia have strengthened. Israel has been able to work productively with Russia. There was the "stabbing Intifada" early in the year 5776 in Israel, but rather than that resulting in an onslaught on Israel, it seems, looking back, to have been more of a harbinger of a new strategy for terror in the West.

Now we come to that "crazy pronouncement" by the educational, scientific, and cultural arm of the UN (UNESCO) to vote to disassociate Israel from the Temple Mount. This is nothing but blatant anti-Semitism, and God Almighty will not ignore this for those fifty nations that voted in favor of it or remained silent. The United States, the UK, and Germany notably stood in opposition to the madness. The vote was planned for summer of 2016, but the Turkish coup attempt against state institutions, including the government and President Recep Erdoğan, surprisingly caused the vote to be held after 5776 was completed, one day *after* the holiest day, Yom Kippur.

Shimon Peres (Photo: Wikicommons)

Finally, in the last days of 5776, the decades-long season of Israeli leaders staking their hopes for peace upon a divided Israel, came to a close. On September 13, 2016, former Prime Minister Shimon Peres had a stroke (strikingly, on the 23rd anniversary of his signing of the Oslo Peace Accords). He died fifteen days later, in time to fit his funeral and remembrance into the last days of 5776. It was widely reported that seventy nations were in attendance. It was less commonly reported that Peres had served in twelve different Israeli administrations.

So has the Jubilee been found? And was Year 5776 a Jubilee?

While 5776 seems to fit the evidence fairly well, it is not a slam dunk. A much better, safer proposition is to say:

We are going through a Jubilee transition!

Rather than focusing on the exact boundaries of the Jubilee year, let us keep watching and investigating, to see what God does between now and the end of 2017. God does not usually fit in the nice, neat boxes in which we vainly try to place Him!

Ultimately, as we stated at the beginning of this book, our goal in trying to solve the Mystery of the Lost Jubilee is to understand the nature of God better. As such, we can safely assume that we will never reach the end of that endeavor, nor would we want to serve a God for which that endeavor could be completed.

A thought for consideration

When it happens, Jubilee is not the same as Messianic deliverance. The Jubilee has to be walked out, lived out. You may get your freedom, but with a few bad decisions you can go right back into slavery. The populist movements in Israel, the United Kingdom, and now the United States would do well to prayerfully remember that.

CHAPTER 29

Looking Back — Was 5777 a Jubilee Year?

NOTE: This chapter was originally published in October 26, 2017.

It has been almost a year since we last wrote on the topic of the Jubilee. Our goal has been to examine the Jubilee year from both Jewish and Christian perspectives. To examine whether God might be restoring to the world the Jubilee calendar as described in Leviticus 25. Since 1967 was a pivotal year in Israel, we thought we should carefully watch 2016 and 2017 for signs of Jubilee.

We began this journey with you nearly two years ago, in November 2015, near the beginning of the year 5776 on the Hebrew calendar. During 5776 (from September 2015 thru October 2016) we wrote the first 27 chapters explaining the background of the Jubilee and looking for evidence that might help us discover whether year 5776 (which mostly falls in 2016) might be a Jubilee year.

Chapter 28, written just after year 5776 ended, suggested that the Jubilee might have been "finally found" as evidenced by three clear sequences of "Jubilee-like" events beginning in Israel, then moving to Great Britain, and finally to America.

(1) In April 2016 (year 5776), Prime Minister Netanyahu declared that the Golan Heights will not be negotiated away

under any circumstances and that it is now officially and eternally a part of Israel. The return of land to its original owners is the key Jubilee-like element we were looking for. Such an event has not happened in Israel since 1967, forty-nine years earlier.

(2) In June of 2016 (also year 5776), the UK voted to exit the European Union, giving it a chance once again to chart its own destiny. Granting freedom to the oppressed is another key Jubilee-like element that we were looking for. This unexpected vote was the biggest news of its kind in decades.

(3) In November 2016 (actually in 5777), the US voted to elect an outsider with no previous political experience as president. Donald Trump ran on a platform of restoring freedom to people who were oppressed and diminished by their own government. It was the biggest surprise event in more than fifty years of American political history. The stock market soared to new heights and many felt like a grand restart was at hand — another key Jubilee-like element.

These three elements (occurring in late 5776 and early 5777) caused us to suggest that, instead of being so concerned about the exact boundaries of these years, we should realize that we were in a "Jubilee season" and that we needed to keep on watching.

This need to "keep watching" is the subject of this chapter.

5777 in Review

So what *has* happened in the last year of 5777, and how does it affect our thinking about the Jubilee?

First, with 5777 now completed, we want to point out again that another year has passed without there being a major war launched against the nation of Israel. We mention this because so many people expected great calamity to befall Israel after the Shemitah and the four Blood Moons ended in fall of 2015. The Gog/Magog war was frequently referenced. We proposed a view opposite to the mainstream opinion — that Israel would likely be entering a great period of prosperity and growth. For the benefit of Israel, we are pleased that this prediction has been the case thus far.

Second, the economic progress worldwide during 5777 was remarkable. Investor confidence has returned with a vengeance, and most economies are growing again. A Jubilee year is a year of rest, but the year following is one of new growth.

Still, the year 5777 was *exactly* fifty years after the great events surrounding the Six Day War and reunification of Jerusalem in 1967 (year 5727). So could 5777 be a Jubilee year?

What were the main Jubilee-like elements found in 5777? The US presidential election in November 2016 has already been mentioned. Besides, that the year was fairly quiet in terms of Jubilee-like elements — especially in Israel. That is, except for one notable development.

The tragic killing of two Druze police officers on the Temple Mount by Palestinian terrorists, followed by the Muslim boycott of their own visits to the Temple Mount, sparked a new resolve and zeal in the Jewish people to begin visiting the Temple Mount once again. The number of Jews who ascended to the Temple Mount during the summer month of Av this year was 4,369 according to the Yeraeh organization, more than double the previous record of any month in Israel's modern history. This trend has continued for three months straight and is "Jubilee-like" in the sense of Jews deciding to "return" to the land they once owned.

Look Up and Look Out!

Additionally, toward the end of 5777, two notable astronomical events occurred that had people talking.

The total solar eclipse on August 21 across the United States had many proposing that great calamity would befall the US. Before the eclipse happened, we suggested a different approach to understanding eclipses in our blog post at https://root-source.com/blog/hype-or-hope-the-total-solar-eclipse-on-august-21-2017/. Indeed, the news on that particular day was good rather than bad, with the biggest news of the day being the location and arrest of the prime suspect in the Barcelona terrorist attacks in Spain.

August 21, 2017, Total Solar Eclipse as Viewed from Wyoming.
(Photo: Andrew Hradesky)

Then, there was the planetary alignment around the constellation Virgo on September 23rd. Again, calamity or a huge step forward in the End Times sequences was often proposed. Before that event occurred we tried to offer a more balanced view in our blog post at https://root-source. com/blog/september-23rd-2017-hype-or-hope-the-revelation-12-controversy/. The days surrounding that event did not deliver much. Overall, it was a much quieter year than many expected.

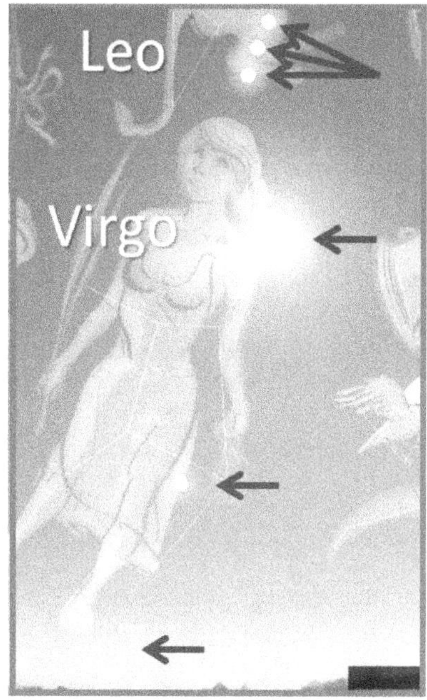

Virgo on September 23, 2017. From top to bottom, arrows point to Venus, Mars, Mercury, the Sun, Jupiter and the Moon. (Photo: Stellarium Software)

Hold that thought

So what can we take from all this regarding the Jubilee and when it might have occured?

From the beginning, we suggested that the period of watching the Jubilee should last until December 31, 2017, rather than ending strictly on the Hebrew calendar year. So, it is still too early to try to look back and assess. We need to wait until January 2018.

See you in three months!

CHAPTER 30

A Lady in Waiting

NOTE: This chapter was written on February 4, 2018.

This journey with you began two years ago in November 2015, near the beginning of the year 5776 on the Hebrew calendar. Now, in year 5778, we are close to wrapping up the book. Our summation chapter is going to reveal a new twist — something we did not expect when we set out on this journey.

Before arriving at our conclusion, we need to bring you up to date on a few things, and offer to you a pair of spectacles (otherwise known today as glasses) to see a few missing facts in the right context.

In all our writings to date regarding Jerusalem, the image of Jerusalem in our minds was the image of the city as surrounded by the walls built by Suleiman the Magnificent, head of the Ottoman Empire.

City of David on the left. Temple Mount on the right. (Photo: Bob O'Dell)

Suleiman conquered the city in 1517 and built the walls between the years of 1536 and 1541. These walls today contain Herod's great platform upon which the Temple stood, bordered by the Western Wall, the holiest site for Jews.

But, in our focus on Jerusalem, we missed discussing something — something important. Can you guess what it is?

The City of David! The original boundaries of Jerusalem were not the boundaries of the Old City today, but further south in what was originally called the City of David. This lower, southern portion of Mount Moriah, that same ridge on which the Temple Mount stands, is accessible by entering the City of David National Park, the place where there is more excavation going on now than in any other archaeological site in the world!

In the Bible, Jerusalem is spoken about as female, not male. This great city, especially the City of David, lay dormant for centuries, waiting for her people to return. Only in the last 150 years has Jerusalem begun to reveal her secrets once again, disclosing them one at a time to careful archaeologists looking to understand her past.

In 1865, Angela Burdett Coutts, a British baroness, visited Jerusalem on a pilgrimage and returned with the idea to establish a Palestine Exploration Fund (PEF), successfully enlisting the help of none other than Queen Victoria. Queen Victoria was mentioned in Chapter 4, but only as an example of a monarch who had celebrated a 50-year Jubilee in her reign, not because we thought Queen Victoria figured into the Jubilee story of Israel.

We were wrong!

How did we discover our omission? Last November 1st, between the 100th anniversary of the Battle of Beersheva and the 100th anniversary of the publication of the Balfour Declaration, we went to the City of David to shoot a video of tour guide AnaRina Heymann (yet another woman in today's story!) guiding us through the city.

She announced that the breakthrough discovery at the site of the City of David was finding the ancient tunnel system that King David may have used to conquer the city. That discovery in 1867 is credited to Charles Warren, who had been commissioned by Queen Victoria and was funded by the PEF, established two years prior by Baroness Coutts.

Queen Victoria (Wikicommons)

Clearly, Queen Victoria was herself a "lady in waiting," waiting to hear reports from Charles Warren on the progress of this important expedition going on in the Holy Land. The Charles Warren letters establish the history of the digs, and the tunnel he found is now part of every City of David Tour.

Tour guide AnaRina went on to tell our group that the 1867 date was, in her opinion, an indication of the repeating 50-year Jubilee cycle, and, of course, she went on to connect that date to the Balfour Declaration in 1917, the Reunification of Jerusalem in 1967, and the very day of our tour. Go to our blog at https://root-source.com/blog/rs-tours-city-of-david-guided-tour-part-1/ to relive that moment with us. We only found out later was that we were hearing her information exactly 150 years (and 8 days) later than the tunnel's discovery by Charles Warren on October 24, 1867.

Why is the Charles Warren discovery in 1867 so important?

First, it falls in the same year that Mark Twain visited the Holy Land and Jerusalem and declared it a desolation. This was covered this extensively in Chapter 15. There we noted that while he visited the land in 1867 — a vote for a 50-year Jubilee cycle — his landmark bestseller *Innocents Abroad* did not reach publication until 1869 — a vote for a 49-year Jubilee cycle. Now we see that Mark Twain and Charles Warren were in Jerusalem at the same time, even if they never met. This strengthens the case for 1867 and for the 50-year Jubilee cycle overall. To recall why a 49-year Jubilee cycle is a viable possibility, reread Chapter 9. But our main point here is that this new information makes the case for the 50-year cycle stronger than we thought.

Second, the involvement of Queen Victoria and Charles Warren in Jerusalem in 1867 strengthens the case for England being part of God's big Jubilee story. Why do we say this? Let's review the facts. Without any doubt, the Jews in Israel were responsible for winning the Six Day War, with God's help. They get the glory of 1967. America played a big role in the UN vote of 1947, establishing the state of Israel. The British, with help from Australia and New Zealand, played the key role in the Balfour Declaration in 1917. We had pegged the key event of 1867 to be once more favoring America, because of the landmark visit of Mark Twain. But this new information about Charles Warren and Queen Victoria gives Britain a similar stake in the key events of 1867. Charles Warren and his team had many discoveries in Jerusalem that year, and they single-handedly inaugurated the modern era of Holy Land archaeology.

The idea that Britain and America might work together in synchronization with a God-ordained Jubilee cycle is a fascinating thought, made possible because of the work of Charles Warren and Queen Victoria.

What's Next?

We promised you a summation article on the Jubilee in early 2018. The end of our journey looks like it is going to arrive at a destination that is bigger and more comprehensive than we expected, so hang on while we finish laying the factual groundwork for you. Don't stop reading now, you're almost there!

CHAPTER 31

When Is for You

NOTE: This chapter was written on February 7, 2018.

That crazy title of this chapter is not a typo, and we will explain later. But first, listen up!

We are close to solving the Mystery of the Lost Jubilee! You have been on a journey with us, as if we were all players in a grand mystery movie. We are at the point in the story where a lead character just proclaimed out loud: "That's it! I know what happened and why!" But, instead of giving the answer right then, he says to his friends, "Come with me!" and walks out of the scene.

This brief gap in the movie serves a purpose. It gives the audience time to reflect on all they have seen — all the facts, all the clues — and to determine if they too are able to view those facts and clues in the same context as the person who claims to have solved the mystery.

FACTS + CLUES + CONTEXT

That is where we are right now in the Jubilee mystery.

And what happens next in our mystery movie? The main character leads us to a place where we have been (perhaps the scene of the crime) and begins to recount facts that are going to be the key to solving the mystery.

That is the purpose of this chapter. We will give you more than just some additional facts. We begin laying out those facts in a way that will get you thinking in the right direction. By the end of this chapter, you will have all the context you need to solve this mystery yourself before you even read the final chapter.

In the concluding chapter, we will offer you a *solution with a twist* — something we did not expect when we set out on this journey. No good mystery movie comes to a close without a final twist at the very end! It must simplify the confusion. It must provide the true motive for what was happening behind the scenes.

Yet, our mystery story is better than the movies. The Mystery of the Lost Jubilee is a real mystery to solve, not a fictional story dreamed up by a great novelist. Our writer is the Writer of all writers — God — and He has a pretty good track record of writing great stories, would you not agree?

The Plot Summary So Far

In this book, we have looked at the Jubilee year from both Jewish and Christian perspectives to examine whether God might be restoring the Jubilee cycle to the world, as it is described in Leviticus 25. After looking back at the amazing and pivotal events of 1967, in the fall of 2015 we invited readers to come with us and watch 2016 and 2017 for signs of Jubilee. We promised to look at the events that happened in those years, and let God show us the answer, by watching what happens. This journey began in November 2015 near the beginning of the year 5776 on the Hebrew calendar and is now coming to a close in February 2018 in year 5778.

The civil new year begins on the Rosh Hashana, the first day of the month of Tishri, the seventh month of the Hebrew calendar. This civil new year (as opposed to the Biblical new year) always comes in the fall, marking the end of the agricultural year and the beginning of a new one. If God's Jubilee is on the Jewish/Hebrew calendar because it deals so directly with the land and its rest, Jews have reasoned that it *must* occur in a year after a Shemitah, just like what happened in 1967. Following that sequence would mean that the Jubilee would begin in fall of 2015 and conclude in fall 2016 (Hebrew calendar year 5776).

But, there was also strong evidence that suggested Jubilee-like events were happening for centuries on years that ended in 17 and 67: 1867, 1917, 1967, etc. This cycle is not related to the Shemitah cycle! So we said that we needed to watch the full calendar year 2017 very closely!

God Plays a Trump Card

Wow! It was a good decision to wait until the end of 2017 before trying to solve this mystery! On December 6, 2017, President Donald Trump announced that the United States would recognize Jerusalem as the capital of Israel and would start the process of relocating its embassy to Jerusalem.

Guatemala quickly joined the US in being the second country to announce a similar move. Incidentally, we wrote about Guatemala's leading role in Christian history in Chapter 14.

While Trump's positive decision toward Jerusalem surprised many around the world, the UN's negative reaction to that announcement did not. On December 21, the UN General Assembly voted to condemn this unilateral action by the United States with a vote of 128 to 9. However, what was not mentioned in most headlines were the 35 abstentions and 21 nations who did not participate in the vote. Thus, a "yes" versus "not yes" tally would actually be a much more respectable 128 to 65.

Few people realize that Russia had actually gone ahead of every other country in the world by declaring West Jerusalem the capital of Israel on April 6, 2017. However, they sided with the Arabs in the December UN vote. Notwithstanding this particular vote, overall relations between Prime Minister Benjamin Netanyahu and Russian President Vladimir Putin and the two countries seem to be improving.

The fact that the United Kingdom sided with most of Europe and the Arab bloc against the US was a big disappointment. However, our perspective is that the United Kingdom is in the middle of negotiations to complete its Brexit, and that getting out of the EU must be its top priority. Readers will remember that we declared the June 2016 Brexit vote as a major indication of God's Jubilee in Chapter 23, second in importance only to Israel's declaration a few months earlier that the Golan Heights were to be forever part of Israel (see Chapter 17).

Will God judge the UK negatively for their vote against Israel? We think not! We believe God understands that now is not the time for the UK to "poke a stick in the eyes" of the very parties from whom it is trying to separate in those negotiations. As Rabbi Ben-Shor told us in Chapter 11, a good judge never judges in isolation. "You have to deal with the reality and the situation as it stands," he said. God is a good judge, not a formula. He understands the UK's present predicament.

But two big questions remain.

First, how positive will Trump's 2017 proclamation be for America? That is the easy one. We believe that God will absolutely bless America for the groundbreaking leadership decision by President Trump. He seems not to have regretted it, reaffirming the decision in his January 30th State of the Union address. He promises Americans that he will pressure other nations to vote with the US in the future or face reduced economic aid packages. Simply put, this one act was *the most positive move* made by a US president toward Israel since President Truman's affirmation of Israel as a nation in 1948. And Trump owns another positive action as well — his decision to visit Israel on his first foreign excursion and while there to pray at the Western Wall.

Yes, Trump will be blessed. All of America will be blessed as well. It does not mean its problems are solved, but America will be unequivocally blessed.

Second, was Trump's action an indication of the timing of God's Jubilee? This is a bit harder. We think, a bit yes and a bit no. Let us be clear that an American declaration concerning the status of Jerusalem as the capital does not change its status in Israel, or in the eyes of God. The United States clearly has no such power. Israel had already declared Jerusalem as its capital 70 years ago; the decision has already been made. In that sense, it is not anything like a Jubilee. However, ever since the Six Day War in June 1967, the United States has slowly begun to turn against Israel in the United Nations. So this declaration, along with the decision that the US would no longer pressure Israel to return to the pre-war 1967 borders, is a departure from the policies of the last 50 years. And as such, it really does seem like a Jubilee — a fresh start — for America, both with respect to its relationship with Israel and with respect to its leadership among the nations. (Reader alert — while we have been slipping you hints in almost every paragraph, we just gave you an especially important one!)

When Is for You!

And now it's time to come back to explain the strange title of this chapter, which also leads us to consider something else: the right context in which to think about the timing of the Jubilee. This strange title "When Is for You" is the amalgamation of a few key words in key verses relating to the Hebrew calendar. Let's discuss the second part first: *"for You."*

When Gidon was in Texas in January 2018, he taught a group Christians, including me (Bob), that the first commandment given to the Jewish people in Exodus is to establish a calendar:

Gidon Ariel (Photo: Bob O'Dell)

> *This month shall be the beginning of months for you; it is to be the first month of the year to you.* (Exodus 12:2)

He explained that the use of the words "for you" and its immediate repetition is so incredibly important, because it indicates that God was willing to *share* the calendar-setting responsibilities with His people. God's calendar was not indiscriminately foisted upon His people. The people participated with God, and He listened and reacted to their judgments. The people had to declare the start of the *month*, and its length, by watching the *moon*. They would declare the start of the *year* by watching the *sun* and its effect on the ripening barley.

This shared responsibility between God and His Jewish people was not unique to this commandment, but that pattern began in that very first commandment listed in Exodus.

A later commandment of God in Leviticus causes us to discuss the first part of our title: "*When.*" When God introduces the Shemitah and the concept of Jubilee in Leviticus 25, He says in verse 2:

> *Speak to the sons of Israel and say to them, "When you come into the land which I shall give you, then the land shall have a sabbath to the Lord."*

First, notice the shared responsibility? The Israelites did not enter the land when they expected to. It was 38 years later. As such, God adjusted His timetable for when the command might be activated. Second, even some 38 years later, God gave them the responsibility to declare "exactly when" they had "officially entered" the land. Jewish tradition (cited in Chapter 16) holds that the Israelites did not declare the "entering" until *after* the seven years it took to conquer the land and *after* the seven years it took to divide the land among the tribes. The exact historical timing is not our point, though. The point is responsibility. They decided *when* to begin to fulfill the counting commandment that is so fundamental to this book:

> *You are also to count off seven sabbaths of years for yourself, seven times seven years, so that you have the time of the seven sabbaths of years, namely, forty-nine years.* (Leviticus 25:8)

It is also clear that the counting is not a decision made individually, nor is it made by a few families. It had to be made on a national scale! It needed full coordination. This is the very issue that the nascent Sanhedrin grappled with when they discussed their rationale to begin the counting in 5776. (Readers: Hint! You might want to reread Chapters 11 and 12).

The last thing we want to mention about our choosing of the title "When Is for You" is to personalize it — for each of us. We said at the beginning of this book that the search to find the Jubilee was like searching for hidden treasure. Proverbs 25:2 reads:

> *It is the glory of God to conceal a matter, but the glory of kings to search it out.*

The search for the "When" is for you — all of you, all of us. God is giving us all the shared responsibility to figure out this mystery, because He knows that there is something valuable and fun and, if we believe it, even *glorious* in the searching for the answer.

Final question for your consideration

We have listed all the facts, we have passed you all our clues, and we have provided all the context you need to solve the mystery for yourself. Would you like to think about it all before turning the page?

When you are ready, our final chapter will reveal our solution — the very last twist in the story — and even predict the future of this wonderful Mystery of the Lost Jubilee.

For those of you who have read every chapter of this book so far, we will use this opportunity to say our goodbyes and thank you for joining. It has been an honor to have you on the journey.

Let the final scene in this mystery movie begin, in *three, two...*

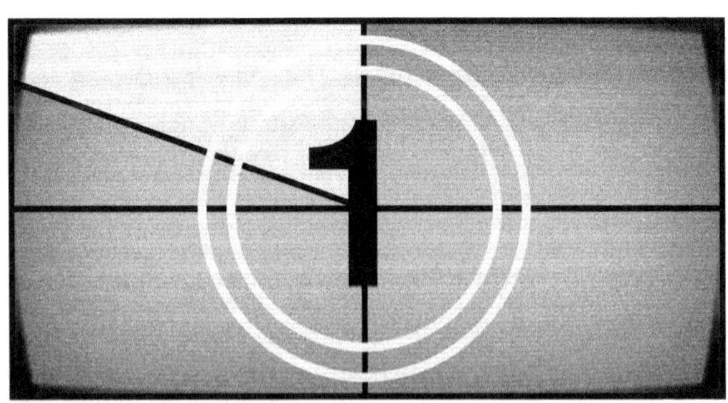

CHAPTER 32

Solved

NOTE: This chapter was written on February 15, 2018.

Two-and-a-half years after we began, it is now time to reveal what we think God has in mind regarding the Jubilee! But first, we will briefly summarize the mystery of the lost Jubilee one final time.

In this book we have looked at the Jubilee year from both Jewish and Christian perspectives to examine whether God might be restoring the Jubilee cycle to the world. After looking back at the amazing and pivotal events of 1967, in fall 2015 we invited readers to come along with us and watch world events during 2015, 2016, and 2017 for signs of the Jubilee. We promised to look at the events in an unbiased manner, like detectives, and let God reveal the answer based on what happens.

On the Hebrew calendar, the civil new year begins in the fall at Rosh Hashana, the first day of the month of Tishri, the seventh month of the Hebrew calendar. We reasoned that if God's Jubilee is on the Jewish/Hebrew calendar, it *must* occur in a year following the land's Sabbatical year, the Shemitah, just as it happened in 1967. Thus, on the Hebrew calendar, the next Jubilee would be 49 years later in year 5776 that began in fall 2015 and concluded fall 2016.

But, there was also strong evidence that suggested Jubilee-like events were happening for centuries on years that ended in 17 and 67: for instance 1867, 1917, 1967, etc. This cycle *is different* from the 49-year Hebrew calendar cycle, *but it converged with the Hebrew calendar cycle perfectly in 1967*! So we agreed to watch the full calendar year 2017 very closely as well, and then decide which Jubilee cycle was the right one. This would solve the Mystery of the Lost Jubilee.

Solved!

The results are all in, and the solution we will propose is definitely not what we expected!

All this time, we have been trying to figure out which cycle is correct — the one embraced by Jews or the one embraced by Gentiles, to see which one is the better fit for the evidence. Instead God has shown us that what he is doing is bigger and more amazing than we thought. This chapter will unveil three surprises for us.

The first surprise is that 1967 was not *just* the year of convergence of the Jewish and Gentile Jubilee cycles, but is the Great Switching Point of Modern History.

> **Surprise #1.** In 1967 the Jubilee train shifted tracks from the pattern of the Gentile Jubilee on the Gregorian calendar, to the pattern of the Jewish Jubilee on the Hebrew calendar.

This is illustrated in the figure below.

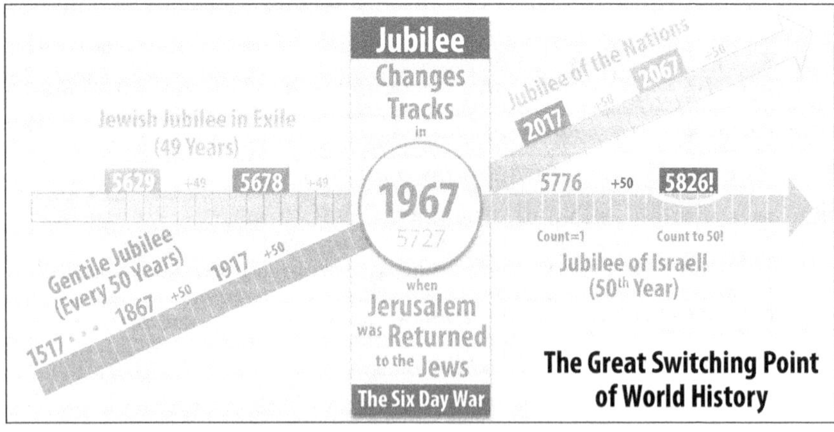

For centuries, God has been continuously working through the Gentile Jubilee pattern, even regarding events that were specifically relevant to the Jews and the Holy Land. Let us review some of the major ones.

The capture of Jerusalem by the Suleiman the Magnificent in 1517 was an early example. Suleiman was friendly and respectful to the Jews and later rebuilt the walls of the Old City of Jerusalem as they stand today. Yet, his actions kicked off a 400-year timer that would eventually end the Turkish rule of Jerusalem in December 1917, when British General Edmund Allenby would capture Jerusalem.

British involvement in the Holy Land actually began fifty years earlier, in 1867 when Queen Victoria asked Charles Warren to begin archaeological excavations of the Old City of Jerusalem. That October, Warren inaugurated the modern age of archaeological exploration of the Holy Land when he discovered the ancient tunnel system near the Gihon Spring in the oldest part of Jerusalem, the City of David.

But the British were not alone in touching the Holy Land in 1867. American Samuel Clemens, aka Mark Twain, visited Jerusalem and the Holy Land that year, turning his notes into what would quickly become the most popular travel book ever written, capturing the hearts and imaginations of people worldwide for a desolate, barren, forsaken land once called Israel.

The British Balfour declaration came 50 years later, signed in the Prime Minister's cabinet room on October 31, 1917, in London — 400 years to the year that Suleiman the Magnificent captured Jerusalem. When Jerusalem surrendered to Allenby in December, the British made clear they were not out to form a new British colony, but to re-establish a homeland for the Jewish people.

Interestingly, the Balfour Declaration was signed 400 years *to the day* after the birth of the Protestant Reformation on October 31, 1517. While the founder of that reformation was inexcusably anti-Semitic, the primary change brought forth by the Protestant Reformation was that Christians began to read the Scriptures for themselves. This began awakening Christians all across Europe to the idea that God was not finished with the Jews and would ultimately restore the Jews to their ancestral homeland. Thus, the Reformation laid the theological groundwork for Christian support of the Jewish return.

Three hundred and fifty years after the Protestant Reformation laid the groundwork, Charles Warren and Mark Twain traveled to Jerusalem in 1867 and commented on the past glories of Jerusalem. Then, fifty years later, in 1917, the British Declaration began the work of creating a homeland for the Jews. But the British would falter in their resolve soon afterward. It would take the grotesque horrors of the Holocaust, combined with American leadership in the UN in November 1947, to propel Israel to become a nation in May 1948.

Until the establishment of Israel, the Jubilee cycle was primarily a Gentile Jubilee. This is not to say God was only interested in the actions of Gentiles. Far from it. But, when significant military or political advancements were made, even if they furthered the Jewish peoples' return, those advancements were usually advised by Jews, but led by Gentiles.

But, 1967 changed everything.

In the spring and summer of 1967, Israel was transformed before the eyes of all nations — tripling its land holdings, reclaiming the Old City of Jerusalem under its sovereignty, and declaring Jerusalem as its eternal capital. The monumental victory was not a Gentile victory, but a Jewish one. The world marveled, and then the very nations who had supported Israel in the past began to turn against her. The UN security council, including the Americans and the British, stood unanimously against Israel's gains from the Six Day War.. Embassies around the world began departing Jerusalem. Israel stood alone.

God looked down and decided it was time for the Jubilee train to switch tracks.

The British Balfour Declaration and British military conquest at the end of the year in 1917 both fell on the Hebrew calendar year 5678 — the first year following the Sabbatical year when the land gets its rest! The Gentile and Jewish Jubilee were therefore synchronized perfectly in 1917. They were perfectly synchronized again in June 1967.

But, what no one realized was that the Jubilee train was switching tracks from the Gentile track of the past to the Jewish track of the future. The switch occurred in 1967 *because this was the first Jubilee Year in which the Jews were back in the land, holding Jerusalem.*

The Jews Have Started the Count!

In the Bible, God gave the Jews the right to decide *when to enter* the land (Leviticus 25:2). He gave them the responsibility to *count* the forty-nine years one by one, (verse 8), and He gave them the honor to *declare* the fiftieth year as a Jubilee by blowing the shofar (verse 9):

> *You shall then sound a ram's horn abroad on the tenth day of the seventh month; on the day of atonement you shall sound a horn all through your land.*

So in hindsight, 1967 would have been the perfect time for the Jews to begin counting off the years of the Jubilee. But, understandably, nobody was thinking about preparing for a Jubilee 50 years into the future at that wild moment. But now they are!

After exactly seven Sabbatical cycles had been completed since the Six Day War, *the Jews counted Year One in 5776.* How **did it** happen? In a small gathering of a few rabbis in Jerusalem between the dates of Rosh Hashana and Yom Kippur, Rabbi Avraham Dov Ben-Shor of the nascent Sanhedrin declared that 5776 was Year One before Almighty God, and prayed:

> *Blessed are you Lord our God, who commands us in the counting of the Sabbaticals and the Jubilees.*

Even though we writers would not learn about this event until several months after we began this journey with you, we saw that their choice to declare 5776 as Year One was perfectly in keeping with the Jewish Jubilee pattern of the Exile we had identified! These same rabbis have also declared Year Two in 5777, and Year Three in 5778, which is the Jewish year at this moment.

We believe that over the next 47 years, their act of counting the years will eventually be accepted by the entire nation of Israel, formally establishing the date of the first official **Jubilee of Israel** to be in year 5826, or fall 2065. Mark your calendars!

The other Jubilee track, the one we have called the Gentile Jubilee, would be better described going forward as the Jubilee of the Nations.

What is going to happen to the Jubilee of the Nations?

Surprise #2. The Jubilee of the Nations may fade away.

Strong Statement. Why?

Because we believe God does not have the intention of maintaining two Jubilee tracks over the long term. The Jubilee is first and foremost about the land of Israel, and the blessing that flows out to the world from Israel. God's wants Israel and the nations to come together, not to walk separately. The fact that the two Jubilee tracks which had been separated for centuries, converged perfectly in 1917 and 1967 establishes God's plan for convergence.

We predict that Israel will declare the first "dry-run" Jubilee of Israel in 5826 (fall 2065). By dry-run, we mean that it will be more of a celebration than a day to implement all of the Jubilee's powerful economic features, such as the clearing of debts and the restoring of land to the original owners. Some of the bigger economic features could be agreed upon in the next 47 years, but those could not realistically be implemented until a second Jubilee occurred almost 100 years from now. However, even if Jews declare a celebratory Jubilee in 47 years, this could cause the unsynchronized Jubilee of the Nations to simply fade into history.

REMINDER: As we already noted in Chapter 27, any predictions we make about future Jubilees assume the Messiah tarries that long, because when the Messiah arrives, he has the authority to declare a year of Jubilee immediately.

And now for the next surprise, possibly the most surprising of all.

Surprise #3. The UK will align itself with Israel very closely in the future, even more closely than the US.

To explain how we came to this, please look at the various Jubilee-related events we have recorded in the last two-and-a-half years.

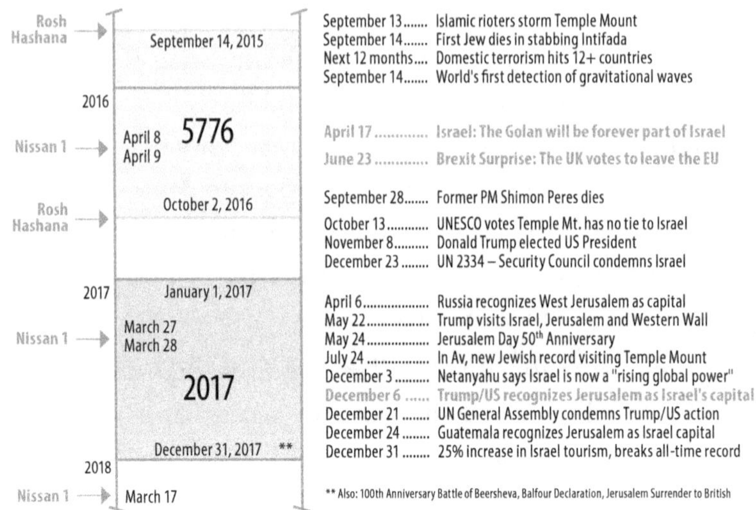

Major Jubilee-Related Events in 2015-2017

The two most dramatic Jubilee-like events occurring in 5776 were on April 17 and June 23. First, Israel declared that the Golan Heights would be forever part of Israel. Prime Minister Netanyahu convened the first-ever official cabinet meeting on the east side of the Jordan river, and stated the Golan was forever being taken off the table for any future peace negotiations. Thus, Israel was officially expanding to the other side of the Jordan river, claiming those lands would be part of Israel forever.

Second, the UK's Brexit vote shocked the world by the decision to leave the European Union. The UK Brexit is a Jubilee-like event because it is a giant national restart, a fresh beginning that allows the people of Britain to be set free from the economic and regulatory bondage of the EU, and begin to live out their own destiny. The EU leadership sneered at this decision, but we believe that the UK will be hugely blessed by its independence, both economically and spiritually.

We see the eventual impact of the UK Brexit will be to bring the UK and Israel together in a big way. With the UK's separation from the EU, it will need to form strong alliances with other partner nations outside of the EU. Israel and the UK are both strong capable democracies, but they are both EU outsiders. Setting aside the current state of their relationship, which is admittedly bad, we believe the pro-Israel community in the UK needs to cheer up, because very good days are ahead. Israel and the UK will be propelled into a strong partnership together, just as those two big Jubilee events came one right after the other.

After the year 5776 ended, Donald Trump was elected US president. While an election is not necessarily a Jubilee, the result of that election was. Once Trump took office in 2017, the year of the Jubilee of the Nations, he visited Jerusalem and the Western Wall in May. In December, he declared Jerusalem to be the capital of Israel, promising to move the US embassy to Jerusalem. In less than three weeks, Guatemala would second the motion. These countries will be blessed for their courage.

The US is the leader of the free world, the leader of nations. But we believe its continued support of Israel will require strong pro-Israel presidents to be elected term after term. But the UK's relationship with Israel will naturally get stronger, regardless of the administration. It will transition from a "nice-to-have" relationship to a "must-have" relationship over time.

The 2017 Jubilee of the Nations Blessed Israel

The Jubilee of the Nations in 2017 was not just about the UK, the US, and Guatemala, it was about all the nations and their relationship to Israel!

In 2017, tourism in Israel broke all-time records, rising an almost unheard of 25% increase year-over-year. In December of 2017, Prime Minister Netanyahu said that the relationship between Israel and the world had changed:

> *The Foreign Ministry carried out a comprehensive survey of 54 countries… The main finding is that in 47 out of 54 countries, a majority of the people there believe that their country would benefit from links with Israel. This is a gigantic change… Israel is a rising global power… Today Israel is a sought-after country. One need only see the 12 hours I was in Africa, or in Latin America on my recent tour there, or on visits to Asia and everywhere else, to see this. Israel is a sought-after, developed and strong country that even the citizens of countries with which we do not have official relations understand the benefit of relations with Israel. We are going from strength to strength and developing even more links.* (Public statement during December 3rd Cabinet meeting)

This remarkable change in outlook took place during 2017, the Jubilee of the Nations. And behind the scenes Arab nations like Saudi Arabia and Egypt came into a closer relationship with Israel as well.

Final Blessing

The Mystery of the Lost Jubilee is the search for whether God is in the process of restoring the Jubilee to Israel *and* to the nations — in other words, to the entire world. Not only is the answer to that question an unequivocal *yes*, but it seems that the best days of the Jubilee — ultimately, God's Jubilee — are still ahead of us. With this truth in mind may all of us, Jew and Gentile, Israel and the nations, join together and proclaim with one voice:

> *Blessed are you Lord our God, King of the Universe, who has created the Sabbaticals and the Jubilees and is in the process of restoring them to the world.*
> ***Amen!***

NOTE: Written on February 15, 2018.

This Appendix is written for those who study the biblical calendar and prefer it over the Jewish civil calendar.

Many people have asked us about whether the Jubilee year should be based on the biblical calendar, the one that God established for the Jews, beginning and ending in spring on Nissan 1. We looked carefully at this issue and have modified our position slightly on one point. But, first let us mention what has not changed.

The Jewish Jubilee (the Jubilee of Israel) does not fit on the biblical calendar for three reasons. First, many people overlook the fact that God speaks of the agricultural year ending in the fall as well as the biblical year ending in spring (see Chapter 24). So there is nothing wrong with the Jubilee year following the pattern of the Sabbatical year, which follows the pattern of the agricultural year cited in Scripture.

Second, if you keep the 49-year cycle as we have, but move the starting/ending dates of the Jubilee back in time six months to the prior Nissan 1, the pivotal events of 1967 fall out of that year, which makes no sense. And if you move the start of the year forward in time six months, the key Jubilee events in 1917 fall out of the year. In short, it just doesn't work.

Third, God gave the Jews the right to proclaim the Jubilee, so we believe He will honor their choice. Their choice is for the year to run from Rosh Hashanah to Rosh Hashanah, and we believe God is respecting that choice. The evidence we found clearly supports this.

But, with regard to the Jubilee of the Nations — defined as beginning on January 1 and ending on December 31 — we have good news for you. It seems like all the data fits for *both* calendars. In other words, with respect to the Jubilee of the Nations, it seems that the key events happen during a nine-month period from Nissan 1 to December 31. Look at the table in Chapter 32 closely and you will see it! Key Jubilee events don't seem to happen in the first 3 months of the Gregorian year!

Perhaps what is going on here is that, God wants as many of His children as possible to see the facts and to come to the same conclusion. This particular finding was so surprising, we were going to include it as the fourth surprise of the final chapter, but then decided against it, due to its technical nature. Nevertheless, we wanted to share it with you in this Appendix.

We will make one final prediction. If God surprises us by allowing the Jubilee of the Nations to survive and thrive in the long term, we believe it will be celebrated on the biblical calendar rather than the Gregorian one, because the biblical calendar creates better alignment between Israel and the nations.

NOTE: Written on March 20, 2018.

After the writing of Appendix A in February 2018 we decided not to send this book out for publication until the current biblical year had ended on Friday at sundown, March 16, 2018. Those few weeks proved interesting due to several events that occurred.

On February 21, 2018, Billy Graham, featured in Chapter 4, passed away. For years, many in the Christian community thought his passing would indicate the end of an era. Even as Shimon Peres passed in the final month of the Jewish Jubilee of 5776, Billy Graham passed in the final month of the Jubilee of the Nations, as we defined it in Appendix A. Both men were honored in life and in death. Both men closed out their own Jubilee years.

On March 8, 2018, President Trump announced his intention to meet North Korean leader Kim Jong-un to begin talks on the denuclearization of North Korea. CNN called the development "a remarkable breakthrough" and reported that President Moon Jae-in of South Korea had recently met with the North Korean leader and said he believed that a "historic" opportunity may be opening up for peace talks. It seems that these events stem from a change of heart from the North Korean leader himself, who said that he would be ceasing further nuclear tests during the interim. If this change of heart persists toward some kind of agreement, we will be able to look back and see its beginning in the final month of the Jubilee of the Nations.

Also, in the last few weeks we learned of significant events occuring in Portugal and Spain. On October 2, 2015, just 19 days into the Jewish Jubilee year, Alfonso Paredes became the first Sephardic Jew to obtain Portuguese citizenship based on a new law which considers the claims of Jews who had their citizenship revoked due to religious persecution in the 15th and 16th centuries, during the Inquisition. In Spain, the enactment of a similar law began on October 1, 2015, also during that same Jubilee Year. Currently, more than 6,000 Jews have been naturalized between these two countries, with more than 12,000 additional applications in process in Portugal alone. How amazing that, after more than 500 years, those severe wrongs would be righted, and the returning of rights once held would occur in the Jewish Jubilee.

These three things together are a final sign, we think, that the Jubilee is fully alive and well in the mind and heart of God.

This Jubilee season is finally recorded. Our story is reaching its final keystroke. But the real story continues on for as far as we can see…

✡   ✡   ✡

…because there is no end to God's heart when it comes to *His* invention, *His* concept, *His* idea, which in English we call the Jubilee and which He originally called *Yovel*.